Thinking Kids™
Carson-Dellosa Publishing LLC
Greensboro, North Carolina

Thinking Kids™
Carson-Dellosa Publishing LLC
P.O. Box 35665
Greensboro, NC 27425 USA

© 2016 Carson-Dellosa Publishing LLC. Except as permitted under the United States Copyright Act, no part of this publication may be reproduced, stored, or distributed in any form or by any means (mechanically, electronically, recording, etc.) without the prior written consent of Carson-Dellosa Publishing LLC. Thinking Kids™ is an imprint of Carson-Dellosa Publishing LLC.

Printed in the USA • All rights reserved.   ISBN 978-1-4838-2696-7
01-015161151

TABLE OF CONTENTS

Math
Multiplication 7
Division 23
Arithmetic 39
Fractions 59
Measurement 75
Time 91

Language Arts
Nouns and Verbs 107
Agreement 123
Adjectives and Adverbs 139
Sentences 155
Vocabulary 171
Punctuation 187
Spelling 203

Answer Key 217

Bonus Activities 244

ABOUT THIS BOOK

Welcome to *Super Skill Powers*, your child's amazing learning adventure! This workbook is unique in that it provides not only valuable practice in standards-based skills but also extra incentive to master them. With the potential to join the superhero team by the end of the book, your child will be determined to succeed!

The engaging comic-book-style format keeps children interested as they advance in their quest for knowledge. Each chapter focuses on a specific skill and culminates in an assessment that gives heroes-in-training immediate feedback on their progress. Each time they succeed on an assessment, students can choose a sticker to outfit their own superhero at the end of the book.

But, the quest doesn't end there. At the end of each chapter, your child can reinforce new knowledge by creating skills-based comic strips. These fun bonus activities encourage children to apply what they've learned in more hands-on and creative ways.

SCORING SYSTEM
To help simplify the scoring process, assessment pages include point bubbles with each set of directions. These tell you how many points are possible in that part of the test. Answers are worth one point each, except for select multi-part answers. The point bubble makes it clear what to count in each section of the test. At the end of the assessment, your child can fill in the total number of correct items in the score burst and then check the guide at the bottom of the page to see if his or her score was high enough to earn a sticker.

BUILDING A SUPERHERO
At the end of the book, your child will find a page of superhero accessory stickers and a card-stock sheet for creating his or her superhero. For best results in building a superhero, your child should add stickers in the order listed below:

1. mask
2. mouth
3. cape
4. shirt
5. pants
6. shorts/skirt
7. belt
8. boot
9. boot
10. glove
11. glove
12. shield
13. shirt decal

MEET THE SUPERHEROES

The Super Skill Squad

Meet the Super Skill Squad! These math and language arts heroes spend their days fighting for knowledge. In their quest to conquer confusion once and for all, they wrestle with numbers, tackle new words, and put unruly letters in their place.

At the Super Skill Squad headquarters, practice is the name of the game. Let these brave masters of learning guide you through the skills you need to become a third-grade superhero. Put in the time and effort to master your skills, and you, too, can be a part of this undefeatable team!

MIGHTY MULTIPLICATION!

Write a multiplication equation to show the number of items in each group. The first one is done for you.

 $3 \times 4 = 12$

_____

_____

_____

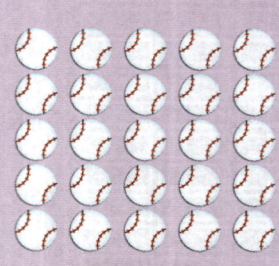

_____

_____

MIGHTY MULTIPLICATION!

Multiply to find each product. Then, draw a line to match each set to the correct multiplication problem. The first one is done for you.

3 × 4 = 12

3 × 3 = ___

2 × 5 = ___

2 × 3 = ___

4 × 2 = ___

6 × 5 = ___

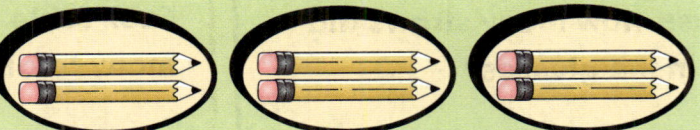

NAME _____

MIGHTY MULTIPLICATION!

Multiply to find each product.

5 × 1 = _____   5 × 5 = _____   3 × 4 = _____

1 × 0 = _____   2 × 2 = _____   4 × 5 = _____

3 × 5 = _____   1 × 1 = _____   2 × 5 = _____

```
  7        4        2        3        4
× 1      × 2      × 3      × 3      × 0
```

Solve each problem.

Maddie has 3 vases with 4 flowers in each vase. How many total flowers does she have?

_____ × _____ = _____ flowers

Mario has 4 packs of gum. There are 5 pieces in each pack. How many pieces of gum does he have?

_____ × _____ = _____ pieces

Jawan has 3 glasses. He put 2 straws in each glass. How many straws did Jawan put in the glasses?

_____ × _____ = _____ straws

We have 4 tables for the party. Each table needs 4 chairs. How many total chairs do we need?

_____ × _____ = _____ chairs

MIGHTY MULTIPLICATION!

Multiply. Use the multiplication chart for help.

x	0	1	2	3	4	5	6	7	8	9
0	0	0	0	0	0	0	0	0	0	0
1	0	1	2	3	4	5	6	7	8	9
2	0	2	4	6	8	10	12	14	16	18
3	0	3	6	9	12	15	18	21	24	27
4	0	4	8	12	16	20	24	28	32	36
5	0	5	10	15	20	25	30	35	40	45
6	0	6	12	18	24	30	36	42	48	54
7	0	7	14	21	28	35	42	49	56	63
8	0	8	16	24	32	40	48	56	64	72
9	0	9	18	27	36	45	54	63	72	81

$$\begin{array}{r} 3 \\ \times 9 \\ \hline \end{array} \qquad \begin{array}{r} 7 \\ \times 6 \\ \hline \end{array}$$

$$\begin{array}{r} 5 \\ \times 4 \\ \hline \end{array} \qquad \begin{array}{r} 7 \\ \times 9 \\ \hline \end{array}$$

$$\begin{array}{r} 8 \\ \times 6 \\ \hline \end{array} \qquad \begin{array}{r} 4 \\ \times 3 \\ \hline \end{array} \qquad \begin{array}{r} 8 \\ \times 5 \\ \hline \end{array} \qquad \begin{array}{r} 4 \\ \times 9 \\ \hline \end{array}$$

$$\begin{array}{r} 3 \\ \times 0 \\ \hline \end{array} \qquad \begin{array}{r} 5 \\ \times 7 \\ \hline \end{array} \qquad \begin{array}{r} 5 \\ \times 1 \\ \hline \end{array} \qquad \begin{array}{r} 4 \\ \times 6 \\ \hline \end{array}$$

$$\begin{array}{r} 8 \\ \times 2 \\ \hline \end{array} \qquad \begin{array}{r} 6 \\ \times 8 \\ \hline \end{array} \qquad \begin{array}{r} 4 \\ \times 0 \\ \hline \end{array} \qquad \begin{array}{r} 3 \\ \times 1 \\ \hline \end{array}$$

$$\begin{array}{r} 6 \\ \times 4 \\ \hline \end{array} \qquad \begin{array}{r} 9 \\ \times 2 \\ \hline \end{array} \qquad \begin{array}{r} 3 \\ \times 4 \\ \hline \end{array} \qquad \begin{array}{r} 6 \\ \times 3 \\ \hline \end{array}$$

NAME _____

MIGHTY MULTIPLICATION!

Time yourself as you solve the problems. Can you answer them correctly in one minute?

9 × 7 = _____		5 × 3 = _____		5 × 4 = _____

4 × 6 = _____		8 × 8 = _____		7 × 7 = _____

8 × 5 = _____		6 × 9 = _____		6 × 8 = _____

2 × 9 = _____		3 × 7 = _____		4 × 4 = _____

Complete each multiplication chart.

×2	
4	
8	
3	6
6	
9	
5	10
7	

×3	
3	9
7	
5	
2	
6	18
4	
8	

×4	
10	
5	20
8	
4	
7	
6	
9	

×5	
9	
2	
6	
3	15
5	
7	
4	

NAME _____

MIGHTY MULTIPLICATION!

Solve each problem.

Steven wants to buy 6 pieces of bubblegum. Each piece costs 5 cents. How much will he have to pay for the bubblegum?

Steven wants to buy _____ pieces of bubblegum.

One piece of bubblegum costs _____ cents.

Steven will have to pay _____ cents total.

There are 7 girls on stage. Each girl is holding 9 flowers. How many flowers are there in all?

There are _____ girls.

Each girl is holding _____ flowers.

There are _____ flowers in all.

There are 4 rows of desks. There are 8 desks in each row. How many desks are there in all?

There are _____ rows of desks.

There are _____ desks in each row.

There are _____ desks in all.

SUPER SKILL POWERS • GRADE 3

NAME _____

MIGHTY MULTIPLICATION!

Multiply. **Tip**: Multiply the bottom number by the tens digit of the top number. Then, add a **0**. The first one is done for you.

30 × 3 = 90	20 × 1		
10 × 9	60 × 4		
80 × 2	40 × 5	50 × 8	90 × 6
40 × 2	80 × 5	90 × 2	10 × 5
20 × 7	50 × 3	70 × 3	20 × 4
10 × 3	90 × 4	70 × 9	60 × 2

14 SUPER SKILL POWERS • GRADE 3

NAME _____

MIGHTY MULTIPLICATION!

Solve each problem.

Gary read 3 books with 60 pages each. How many pages did he read in all?

There are _____ pages in each book.

Gary read _____ books.

Gary read _____ pages in all.

There are 4 classes at a school. Each class has 20 students. How many students are at the school?

There are _____ students in each class.

There are _____ classes.

There are _____ students in the school.

Yolanda used up 4 rolls of stickers. If each roll has 30 stickers, how many stickers did she use in all?

Each roll has _____ stickers.

Yolanda used _____ rolls.

Yolanda used a total of _____ stickers.

There are 10 apples in each basket. If Mary buys 6 baskets, how many apples does she have?

Mary has _____ apples.

During a game, 2 teams play against each other. There are 10 players on the field for each team. How many players are on the field during the game?

There are _____ players on the field.

NAME _____

MIGHTY MULTIPLICATION!

Find the value of **?** in each problem below.

$6 \times (5 \times ?) = (6 \times 5) \times 12$

? = _____

$(? \times 9) \times 3 = 16 \times (9 \times 3)$

? = _____

$(5 \times 8) \times 10 = 5 \times (? \times 10)$

? = _____

$2 \times (? \times 6) = (2 \times 14) \times 6$

? = _____

$(? \times 6) \times 11 = 9 \times (6 \times 11)$

? = _____

$5 \times (5 \times ?) = (5 \times 5) \times 8$

? = _____

$(14 \times ?) \times 6 = 14 \times (3 \times 6)$

? = _____

$20 \times (4 \times 7) = (? \times 4) \times 7$

? = _____

NAME _____

MIGHTY MULTIPLICATION!

Numbers can be multiplied in different ways to get the same product. Write a product in each blank.

(2 × 3) × 4 = 24

6 × 4 = _____

3 × 6 = 18

6 × 3 = _____

(3 × 4) + (3 × 2) = 18

3 × (4 + 2) = _____

15 × 2 = 30

2 × 15 = _____

(6 × 2) × 4 = 48

12 × 4 = _____

5 × (4 + 4) = 40

(5 × 4) + (5 × 4) = _____

Use the distributive property to make the problems easier to solve. The first one is done for you.

9 × 15 =
(9 × 10) + (9 × 5) = 135

8 × 22 =
(8 × ___) + (8 × ___) = _____

14 × 8 =
(___ × 8) + (___ × 8) = _____

18 × 6 =
(___ × 6) + (___ × 6) = _____

20 × 12 =
(20 × ___) + (20 × ___) = _____

8 × 16 =
(8 × ___) + (8 × ___) = _____

SUPER SKILL POWERS • GRADE 3   17

ASSESSMENT: MULTIPLICATION

Write a multiplication equation to show the number of items in each group.

2 pts

_____

_____

Solve each problem.

4 pts

Ian has 4 bags. He puts 9 marbles in each bag. How many marbles are there in all?

_____ × _____ = _____ marbles

Jennifer jumped over 7 rocks. She jumped over each rock 4 times. How many times did she jump in all?

_____ × _____ = _____ times

Thirty students each have a button collection. Each collection contains 8 buttons. How many buttons do the students have altogether?

_____ × _____ = _____ buttons

The computer classroom has 6 rows of computers. There are 5 computers in each row. How many computers are in the classroom total?

_____ × _____ = _____ computers

NAME _____

ASSESSMENT: MULTIPLICATION

Solve using the distributive property. **2 pts**

$17 \times 2 =$
$(8 \times 2) + (\underline{} \times 2) = \underline{}$

$15 \times 4 =$
$(10 \times 4) + (\underline{} \times 4) = \underline{}$

Multiply. **18 pts**

8 × 3	4 × 9	9 × 9	6 × 8	5 × 7
4 × 4	6 × 0	8 × 5	0 × 9	10 × 2
7 × 1	40 × 3	90 × 2	50 × 5	
7 × 7	20 × 8	60 × 2	70 × 3	

YOUR SCORE ___ / 26

21–26 CORRECT ANSWERS = 1 STICKER

NAME _____

BONUS MULTIPLICATION!

Draw groups of objects, animals, or people in each comic book frame. For each group, count how many items there are, and then write an equation that multiplies that number by another number from 0 to 10. If they will fit, draw the resulting number of items in the box.

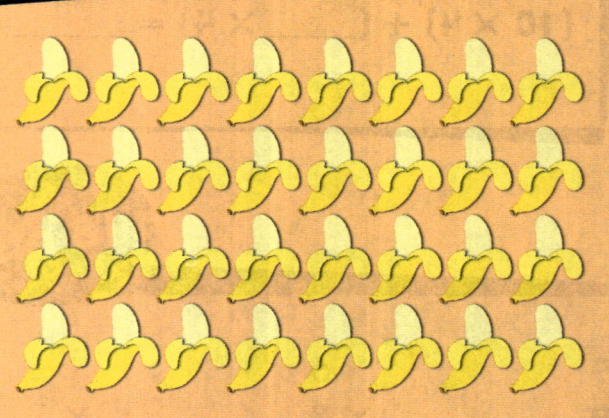

8 × 4 = 32

SUPER SKILL POWERS • GRADE 3

NAME _____

BONUS MULTIPLICATION!

NAME _____

BONUS MULTIPLICATION!

NAME _____

DYNAMIC DIVISION!

Use the information on the bar graph to write the answers to the questions.

Make 3 equal groups.

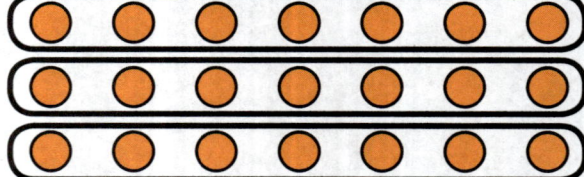

How many are in each group? 7

Make 5 equal groups.

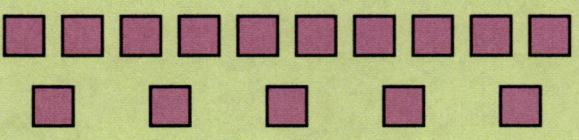

How many are in each group? ____

Make 2 equal groups.

How many are in each group? ____

Make 4 equal groups.

How many are in each group? ____

Make 5 equal groups.

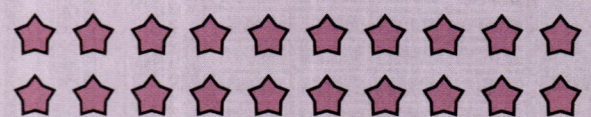

How many are in each group? ____

Make 6 equal groups.

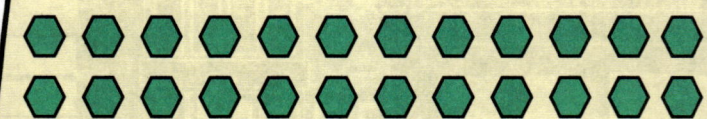

How many are in each group? ____

NAME _____

DYNAMIC DIVISION!

Divide each set of objects into 2 equal groups. Then, divide to find each quotient.

6 ÷ 2 = _____

4 ÷ 2 = _____

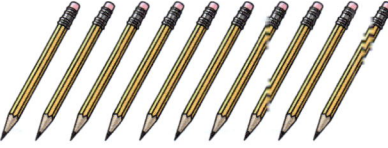

10 ÷ 2 = _____

8 ÷ 2 = _____

Divide each set of objects into 3 equal groups. Then, divide to find each quotient.

15 ÷ 3 = _____

21 ÷ 3 = _____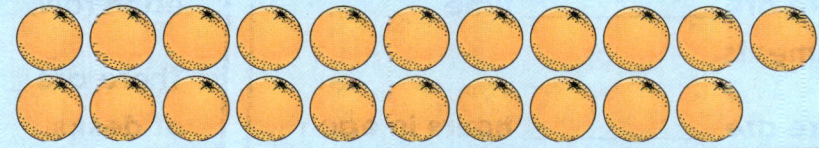

9 ÷ 3 = _____

NAME _____

DYNAMIC DIVISION!

Divide to find each quotient.

3)18   4)24   3)21   4)36   8)32

5)40   6)36   9)36   8)40   9)27

Solve each problem.

There are 24 hours in a day. If the day is divided into 6 equal time segments, how many hours will be in each time segment?

There are _____ hours.

There are _____ time segments.

There are _____ hours in each time segment.

There are 30 desks in the classroom. There are 6 desks in each row. How many rows of desks are there?

There are _____ desks.

There are _____ desks in each row.

There are _____ rows of desks.

26 SUPER SKILL POWERS • GRADE 3

DYNAMIC DIVISION!

Use the fact family in each square to make number sentences.

3, 6, 18

____ × ____ = ____

____ × ____ = ____

____ ÷ ____ = ____

____ ÷ ____ = ____

9, 4, 36

____ × ____ = ____

____ × ____ = ____

____ ÷ ____ = ____

____ ÷ ____ = ____

6, 8, 48

____ × ____ = ____

____ × ____ = ____

____ ÷ ____ = ____

____ ÷ ____ = ____

Answer each question.

How many 6s are in 18? _____

How many 5s are in 25? _____

How many 2s are in 8? _____

How many 4s are in 20? _____

How many 7s are in 42? _____

How many 9s are in 18? _____

How many 7s are in 21? _____

How many 8s are in 32? _____

How many 6s are in 36? _____

How many 3s are in 15? _____

DYNAMIC DIVISION!

Time yourself as you solve the problems. Can you answer them correctly in one minute?

25 ÷ 5 = _____   72 ÷ 8 = _____   81 ÷ 9 = _____

28 ÷ 4 = _____   36 ÷ 6 = _____   56 ÷ 8 = _____

12 ÷ 2 = _____   45 ÷ 5 = _____   32 ÷ 8 = _____

21 ÷ 3 = _____   18 ÷ 3 = _____   63 ÷ 9 = _____

14 ÷ 7 = _____   30 ÷ 5 = _____   49 ÷ 7 = _____

Divide.

2)84   2)62   2)68   3)93

7)70   5)55   3)69   9)99

3)36   9)90   3)42   4)80

DYNAMIC DIVISION!

Solve each problem.

Spencer wants to save 72 dollars. How many weeks will it take Spencer to save 72 dollars if he saves 9 dollars each week?

Spencer wants to save _____ dollars.

He saves _____ dollars each week.

It will take Spencer _____ weeks to save 72 dollars.

Ms. Jefferson worked 40 hours this week. She worked 8 hours each day. How many days did she work this week?

Ms. Jefferson worked _____ hours this week.

She worked _____ hours each day.

She worked _____ days this week.

There are 16 football players on the field. If there are 8 players on each team, how many teams are on the field?

There are _____ football players on the field.

There are _____ players on each team.

There are _____ teams on the field.

Mrs. Daniels ordered 63 chairs and 7 tables for a banquet. Each table will have the same number of chairs. How many chairs will be at each table?

There will be _____ chairs at each table.

DYNAMIC DIVISION!

Use the fact family in each square to make number sentences. The first one is done for you.

2 | 10 | 20

 2 × 10 = 20
10 × 2 = 20
20 ÷ 10 = 2
20 ÷ 2 = 10

5 | 10 | 50

___ × ___ = ___
___ × ___ = ___
___ ÷ ___ = ___
___ ÷ ___ = ___

8 | 10 | 80

___ × ___ = ___
___ × ___ = ___
___ ÷ ___ = ___
___ ÷ ___ = ___

4 | 10 | 40

___ × ___ = ___
___ × ___ = ___
___ ÷ ___ = ___
___ ÷ ___ = ___

7 | 10 | 70

___ × ___ = ___
___ × ___ = ___
___ ÷ ___ = ___
___ ÷ ___ = ___

9 | 10 | 90

___ × ___ = ___
___ × ___ = ___
___ ÷ ___ = ___
___ ÷ ___ = ___

DYNAMIC DIVISION!

Divide. Under each division problem, write the corresponding multiplication problem. The first one is done for you.

7)7̄   6)24   8)56   6)30   8)64
7 × 1 = 7

6)12   7)35   8)24   7)28   6)36

Divide.

9)63   9)81   7)56   5)35   8)24

9)18   7)14   7)21   8)48   9)45

DYNAMIC DIVISION!

Write a number in the burst to complete each equation.

56 ÷ ____ = 8

35 ÷ ____ = 5

____ ÷ 9 = 2

____ ÷ 7 = 3

28 ÷ 7 = ____

20 ÷ 4 = ____

____ ÷ 9 = 10

____ ÷ 6 = 6

40 ÷ ____ = 8

100 ÷ ____ = 10

NAME _____

DYNAMIC DIVISION!

Draw a line to match each related division and multiplication problem.

65 ÷ 5 •	• 9 × 4
24 ÷ 6 •	• 6 × 4
36 ÷ 9 •	• 9 × 5
45 ÷ 5 •	• 17 × 3
28 ÷ 7 •	• 7 × 4
64 ÷ 8 •	• 9 × 9
51 ÷ 3 •	• 8 × 8
81 ÷ 9 •	• 13 × 5
72 ÷ 9 •	• 18 × 4
38 ÷ 2 •	• 8 × 9
72 ÷ 4 •	• 22 × 4
50 ÷ 2 •	• 19 × 2
56 ÷ 4 •	• 43 × 2
86 ÷ 2 •	• 25 × 2
88 ÷ 4 •	• 14 × 4
75 ÷ 3 •	• 25 × 3

NAME _____

ASSESSMENT: DIVISION

Divide each set of objects into equal groups. Then, divide to find the quotient.

2 pts

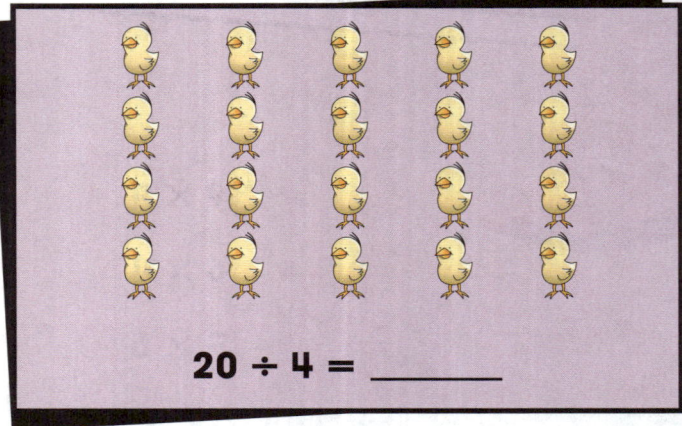

20 ÷ 4 = _____

15 ÷ 5 = _____

Solve each problem.

4 pts

There are 64 pages in a book. There are 8 chapters in the book. Each chapter has the same number of pages. How many pages are in each chapter of the book?

There are _____ pages in each chapter of the book.

A golfer shot a score of 45 in a golf match. She played 9 holes. She had the same score at each hole. What was her score at each hole?

She shot a score of _____ at each hole.

Seventy-two teenagers went on a river-rafting trip. If each raft held 8 teenagers, how many rafts did the teenagers have for their trip?

The teenagers had _____ rafts.

Six horses can live in the stable. If 1 horse can live in each stall, how many stalls are in the stable?

There are _____ stalls in the stable.

ASSESSMENT: DIVISION

NAME _____

Use the fact family in each square to make number sentences.   **3 pts**

Square 1: 8, 3, 24
- ___ × ___ = ___
- ___ × ___ = ___
- ___ ÷ ___ = ___
- ___ ÷ ___ = ___

Square 2: 7, 9, 63
- ___ × ___ = ___
- ___ × ___ = ___
- ___ ÷ ___ = ___
- ___ ÷ ___ = ___

Square 3: 6, 10, 60
- ___ × ___ = ___
- ___ × ___ = ___
- ___ ÷ ___ = ___
- ___ ÷ ___ = ___

Divide.   **15 pts**

2)14	2)10	1)3	4)20	3)18	8)72
2)6	7)56	3)24	4)32	7)63	
4)16	8)32	5)30	9)81		

YOUR SCORE ___ / 24

19–24 CORRECT ANSWERS = 1 STICKER

BONUS DIVISION!

Practice dividing sets of even-numbered objects into equal groups. Draw even numbers of objects you see around the neighborhood. Then, circle items in the set to make equal groups. Finally, write the division problem your drawing shows.

$20 \div 5 = 4$

NAME _____

BONUS DIVISION!

NAME _____

BONUS DIVISION!

NAME _____

OUTRAGEOUS ARITHMETIC!

Add.

```
  63      13      47      19      63
 +29     +37     +23     +29     +21


  31      20      49      33      46
 + 5     + 0     +26     +44     +53


  86      75      63      11      16
 + 5     + 6      19      22      32
                 + 8     +33     +11
```

Subtract.

```
  93      76      82      67      14
 - 5     -13     -45     -41     -12


  87      28      65      57      63
 -19     -13     -42     -35     -14
```

NAME _____

OUTRAGEOUS ARITHMETIC!

Solve each problem.

At an air show there were 32 airplanes in the sky. If 15 airplanes landed, how many were still in the sky?

There were _____ airplanes still in the sky.

One bag of rocks weighs 15 pounds. Another bag of rocks weighs 23 pounds. How much do both bags of rocks weigh?

Together, the bags of rocks weigh _____ pounds.

The car dealer had 17 model cars. Yesterday, he sold 9 of the model cars. How many model cars does he have left?

The car dealer has _____ model cars left.

There were 46 people at the train station. Then, 27 people got on the train. How many people are still at the train station?

There are _____ people still at the train station.

Beatrix invited 26 people to her party. Only 9 people cannot come to the party. How many people will be at Beatrix's party?

There will be _____ people at Beatrix's party.

OUTRAGEOUS ARITHMETIC!

Add or subtract.

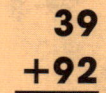

39 +92	86 +93	132 − 41	186 − 92	543 −121

192 + 76	154 − 92	543 −206	150 − 90	650 +129

137 +310	159 − 82	185 − 96	432 −257	710 −512

541 +862	432 −119	720 +140	186 −107	540 − 75

812 + 93	712 −347	690 −320	451 −253	512 −308

119 +104	703 +219	861 −172	186 +210	513 −211

OUTRAGEOUS ARITHMETIC!

Solve each problem.

Kurt has saved 29 dollars to buy a remote control car. The remote control car that he wants to buy costs 43 dollars. How much more money does he need to save?

Are you to add or subtract? _____

He will need to save _____ more dollars.

Latisha sold 136 candy bars on Friday and 245 candy bars on Saturday. How many candy bars did she sell in all?

Are you to add or subtract? _____

Latisha sold _____ candy bars in all.

Tawna has 253 pennies. Shawn has 146 pennies. How many more pennies does Tawna have than Shawn?

Tawna has _____ more pennies than Shawn.

Harry had 257 pennies and 316 dimes. How many coins does he have?

Are you to add or subtract? _____

He has _____ coins.

The team sold 453 tickets for the game. There were 249 adult tickets sold. How many children's tickets were sold?

The team sold _____ children's tickets.

SUPER SKILL POWERS • GRADE 3   43

NAME _____

OUTRAGEOUS ARITHMETIC!

Write each number sentence. Put a box (□) in the sentence for the missing part. Then, solve. The first one is done for you.

The sum of two and three is what number?   2 + 3 = □

The sum of two and three is _____five_____.

Seven minus two is what number? _____

Seven minus two is _____.

Four times three is what number? _____

Four times three is _____.

Fourteen divided by two is what number? _____

Fourteen divided by two is _____.

Five added to what number is seven? _____

Five added to _____ is seven.

Thirteen minus what number is ten? _____

Thirteen minus _____ is ten.

This number times five is twenty-five. _____

_____ times five is twenty-five.

This number divided by seven is nine. _____

_____ divided by seven is nine.

NAME _____

OUTRAGEOUS ARITHMETIC!

Write each number sentence. Put a box (□) in the sentence for the missing part. Then, solve.

Twenty-seven divided by a number equals three. _____

Twenty-seven divided by _____ equals three.

This number divided by eight equals eight. _____

_____ divided by eight equals eight.

Twelve divided by three equals what number? _____

Twelve divided by three equals _____ .

Four times nine is what number? _____

Four times nine is _____ .

This number times eight is fifty-six. _____

_____ times eight is fifty-six.

Nine times this number is eighty-one. _____

Nine times _____ is eighty-one.

Twenty divided by four is what number? _____

Twenty divided by four is _____ .

Ten times this number is ninety. _____

Ten times _____ is ninety.

SUPER SKILL POWERS • GRADE 3   45

OUTRAGEOUS ARITHMETIC!

Use addition, subtraction, multiplication, or division to solve each problem.

Owen is going to visit his aunt. He travels 278 miles on Saturday. He travels 81 miles farther on Sunday than he did on Saturday. How many miles did Owen travel on Sunday?

Owen traveled _____ miles on Sunday.

In the year 1983, Mr. Smith was 94 years old. In what year was he born?

Mr. Smith was born in the year _____.

Marcella has a dog-walking business. She walked 12 dogs on Thursday, 15 dogs on Saturday, and 9 dogs on Sunday. How many dogs did Marcella walk altogether?

Marcella walked _____ dogs altogether.

There are 36 students who live in the college dormitory. If 4 students live in each room, how many rooms are there in the dormitory?

There are _____ rooms in the dormitory.

Joe's fish store has 18 goldfish. The fish are in 3 aquariums. The same number of goldfish are in each aquarium. How many goldfish are in each aquarium?

There are _____ goldfish in each aquarium.

NAME _____

OUTRAGEOUS ARITHMETIC!

Use addition, subtraction, multiplication, or division to solve each problem. One problem takes two different operations.

Last week, the ice cream shop sold 188 hot fudge sundaes, 54 chocolate sundaes, and 62 strawberry sundaes. How many more hot fudge sundaes did the store sell than chocolate and strawberry combined?

The store sold _____ more hot fudge sundaes than all the others combined.

Tito read 320 pages in a book. Akando read 323 pages in a book. Kenji read 313 pages in a book. How many pages did they read altogether?

Tito, Akando, and Kenji read _____ pages.

Eight people paid a total of 24 dollars for admission into the school carnival. If each ticket cost the same amount, how much did each ticket cost?

The cost of each ticket was _____ dollars.

A family of 5 takes an ice chest to the beach. There are 10 water bottles in the ice chest. How many water bottles will each person receive if each person receives the same number of water bottles?

Each person will receive _____ water bottles.

Elisa has 15 sticks of gum. If she gives each of her 3 friends the same number of sticks of gum, how many sticks of gum will each of Elisa's friends have?

Each of Elisa's friends will have _____ sticks of gum.

OUTRAGEOUS ARITHMETIC!

Solve each problem.

| 2)22 | 16 ×6 | 3)63 | 3)27 | 46 −28 |

| 38 +17 | 83 −47 | 57 +34 | 18 ×4 | 24 ×3 |

| 2)56 | 7)70 | 804 −238 | 132 −78 | 176 +394 |

| 52 11 +26 | 12 ×8 | 9)81 | 479 +277 | 921 −643 |

NAME _____

OUTRAGEOUS ARITHMETIC!

Solve each problem.

$9\overline{)99}$ 13 $2\overline{)44}$ $11\overline{)55}$ 389
           × 3   − 92

413   886   575   25   17
+508   −347   +223   × 4   × 5

$6\overline{)78}$ $5\overline{)50}$ 710   107   929
                             −119   + 93   −105

27   16 $3\overline{)66}$ 561   662
38   × 4   +239   −378
+14

NAME _____

OUTRAGEOUS ARITHMETIC!

Solve each problem using two different operations.

Emma has 50 photos in one box and 10 photos in another. She wants to put an equal number of photos on each of the 10 pages of her album. How many photos should Emma put on each page?

Emma should put _____ pictures on each page.

A group of 10 third graders are making cardboard penguins. Each student needs 1 cardboard tube, 2 wiggle eyes, and 1 piece of construction paper. How many items total do all 10 third graders need?

All 10 third graders need _____ items for the penguin project.

Greg has 91 erasers, and Janelle gives him 8 more. Greg gives each of his 9 friends an equal number of erasers. How many erasers does each friend get?

Each friend gets _____ erasers.

There were two lines for the ski lift. Twenty-one skiers were waiting in one line, and 12 were waiting in the other. Three skiers can sit on each seat on the lift. How many seats are needed for all of the skiers?

_____ seats are needed for all of the skiers.

NAME _____

OUTRAGEOUS ARITHMETIC!

It takes two steps to find the solution to each problem below. Write both equations you use to find each solution. The first one is done for you.

Ezra has $20. He buys 3 fossils for $3 each. How much money does he have left?

$3 × \$3 = \$9$ $\$20 - \$9 = \$11$

Zoe had a garden party with 6 friends. Each friend got 2 packets of flower seeds to take home. Zoe kept 4 packets of seeds for her own garden. How many packets of flower seeds were there in all?

_____ _____

Azim had 55 grapes. He fed his 8 chickens 6 grapes each. How many grapes were left?

_____ _____

Kendall's mom makes picnic blankets. She can make 9 blankets with 27 yards of fabric. How much fabric would she need to make 12 blankets?

_____ _____

SUPER SKILL POWERS • GRADE 3 **51**

NAME _____

OUTRAGEOUS ARITHMETIC!

Complete each number sentence. The first one is done for you.

$0 + 4 = \boxed{4}$ $0 + 6 = \square$ $\square + 2 = 2$

$1 \times 2 = \square$ $1 \times 5 = \square$ $\square \times 4 = 4$

$7 + 2 = \square + 7$ $3 + 4 = \square + 3$ $1 + 2 = 2 + \square$

$5 \times 7 = 7 \times \square$ $4 \times \square = 3 \times 4$ $\square \times 3 = 3 \times 5$

Complete the following. The first one is done for you.

$2 + 7 = 9$ or
$2 + 7 = 5 + \boxed{4}$

$5 + 7 = 12$ or
$5 + 7 = 6 + \square$

$4 + 3 = 7$ or
$4 + 3 = 5 + \square$

$6 + 4 = 10$ or
$6 + 4 = 5 + \square$

$6 + 7 = 13$ or
$6 + 7 = 8 + \square$

$5 + 3 = 8$ or
$5 + 3 = 6 + \square$

$5 \times 6 = 30$ or
$5 \times 6 = 10 \times \square$

$4 \times 3 = 12$ or
$4 \times 3 = 2 \times \square$

$6 \times 3 = 18$ or
$6 \times 3 = 9 \times \square$

OUTRAGEOUS ARITHMETIC!

Solve using the associative property. The first one is done for you.

$3 \times 5 \times 2 = d$

$\underline{3} \times \underline{5} = \underline{15}$
$\underline{15} \times \underline{2} = \underline{d}$
$d = \underline{30}$

$2 \times 9 \times 1 = h$

___ × ___ = ___
___ × ___ = ___
$h = $ ___

$4 \times 6 \times 2 = e$

___ × ___ = ___
___ × ___ = ___
$e = $ ___

$7 \times 4 \times 2 = g$

___ × ___ = ___
___ × ___ = ___
$g = $ ___

Solve using the distributive property. The first one is done for you.

$12 \times 4 = (6 \times 4) + (\underline{6} \times 4)$
$\underline{24} + \underline{24}$
$12 \times 4 = \underline{48}$

$14 \times 3 = (8 \times 3) + (\underline{} \times 3)$
___ + ___
$14 \times 3 = $ ___

$19 \times 2 = (9 \times 2) + (\underline{} \times 2)$
___ + ___
$19 \times 2 = $ ___

$16 \times 5 = (7 \times 5) + (\underline{} \times 5)$
___ + ___
$16 \times 5 = $ ___

ASSESSMENT: ARITHMETIC

Solve each problem using two different operations. **4 pts**

Kiri has 10 friends from school and 6 friends from her neighborhood. She gave each friend 2 apples. How many apples did Kiri have?

Kiri had _____ apples.

Two of Mr. Black's daughters need new sneakers. The other two daughters need new dress shoes. Each pair of shoes will cost 30 dollars. How much money will Mr. Black spend on shoes for his daughters?

Mr. Black will spend _____ dollars on shoes.

There are 7 friends that each had 3 dollars. One friend gave away 2 dollars. How much money do the 7 friends have total?

The friends have a total of _____ dollars.

Jamal invited 40 people to his party. Eight people said they could not come. If Jamal makes 96 cookies for his guests, how many cookies will each guest get if they are split up equally?

Each guest at Jamal's party will get _____ cookies.

Complete the following. **4 pts**

$0 + 8 = \square$

$\square \times 4 = 4$

$9 + 5 = \square + 9$

$6 \times 7 = 7 \times \square$

Solve using the associative or distributive property. **2 pts**

$5 \times 5 \times 2 = y$

$y = \_\_\_\_$

$18 \times 4 = (8 \times 4) + (\_\_\_\_ \times 4)$

$18 \times 4 = \_\_\_\_$

ASSESSMENT: ARITHMETIC

Solve each problem.

20 pts

$7\overline{)70}$ 12×6 $3\overline{)36}$ $11\overline{)66}$ $240 + 125$

$679 - 336$ $348 - 123$ $568 + 193$ 30×5 16×3

$7\overline{)91}$ $3\overline{)75}$ $875 - 241$ $271 + 378$ $572 - 320$

$43\ 19 + 21$ 21×4 $4\overline{)92}$ $435 + 281$ $756 - 110$

YOUR SCORE ___/30

24–30 CORRECT ANSWERS = 1 STICKER

NAME _____

BONUS ARITHMETIC!

Practice using the four operations to solve problems. Write a number between 0 and 100 in each comic strip frame. Then, see how many different equations you can write that give you that number as an answer.

32

$64 - 32 = 32$

$16 + 16 = 32$

$8 \times 4 = 32$

$96 \div 3 = 32$

NAME _____

BONUS ARITHMETIC!

NAME _____

BONUS ARITHMETIC!

NAME _____

FANTASTIC FRACTIONS!

Follow the directions to divide the shapes into fractions.

Draw lines to divide the circle into four equal parts. What is one part called?

_____

Draw a line to divide the triangle into two equal parts. What is one part called?

_____

Draw lines to divide the rectangle into three equal parts. What is one part called?

_____

The fraction $\frac{3}{1}$ is the same as the whole number 3. Write numbers in the boxes to make a fraction that shows each whole number.

NAME _____

FANTASTIC FRACTIONS!

Draw lines to divide each shape according to the fraction given.

thirds    fourths    fifths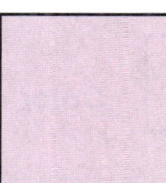

eighths    halves 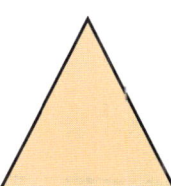   tenths

Follow the directions to color equal parts of the shapes.

Color one fourth.
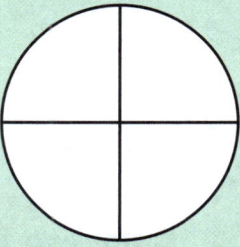

Color two thirds.
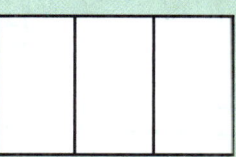

Color four fourths.
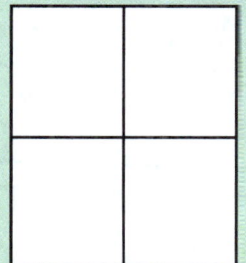

Color one third.
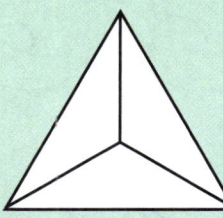

Color one half.

Color three fourths.
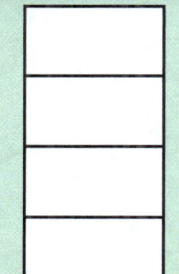

NAME _____

FANTASTIC FRACTIONS!

Color the objects to show each fraction. The first one is done for you.

$\frac{1}{3}$ Color one-third.	$\frac{2}{4}$ Color two-fourths.	$\frac{3}{6}$ Color three-sixths.
		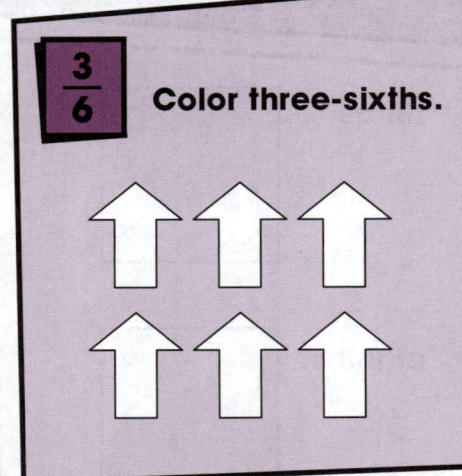
$\frac{1}{6}$ Color one-sixth.	$\frac{1}{4}$ Color one-fourth.	$\frac{5}{8}$ Color five-eighths.
		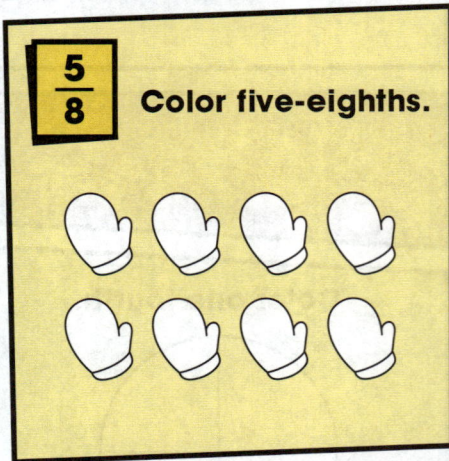
$\frac{3}{4}$ Color three-fourths.	$\frac{1}{2}$ Color one-half.	$\frac{2}{3}$ Color two-thirds.
		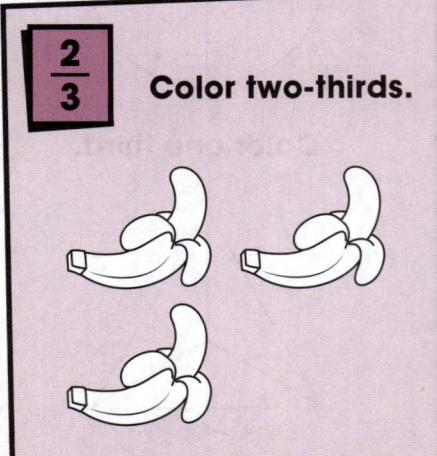

FANTASTIC FRACTIONS!

Color the objects to show each fraction.

1/8 Color one-eighth.

3/4 Color three-fourths.

1/3 Color one-third.

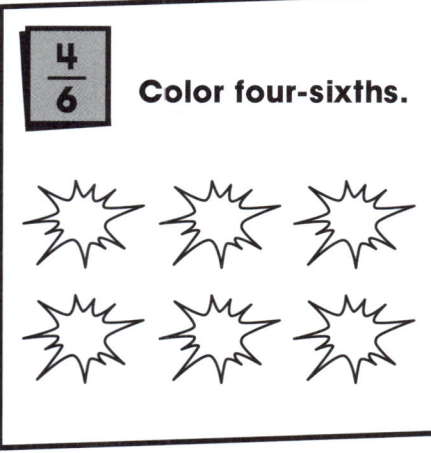
4/6 Color four-sixths.

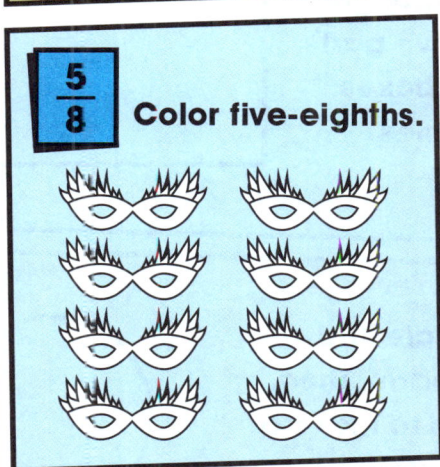
5/8 Color five-eighths.

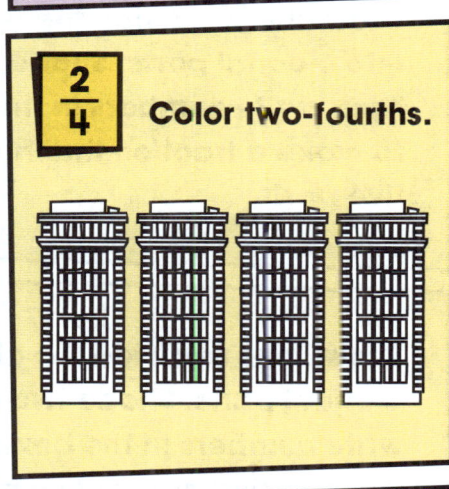
2/4 Color two-fourths.

3/8 Color three-eighths.

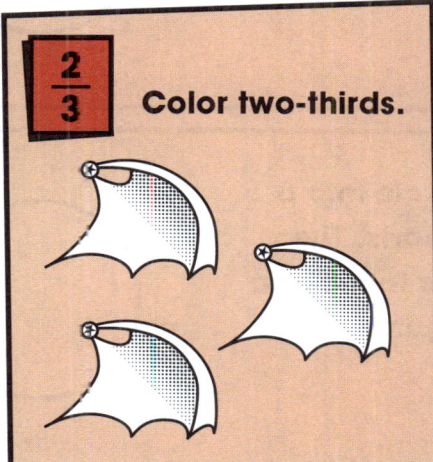
2/3 Color two-thirds.

3/6 Color three-sixths.

SUPER SKILL POWERS • GRADE 3   63

NAME _____

FANTASTIC FRACTIONS!

Follow the directions.

Draw lines to divide the square into 4 equal parts. Shade one part. Then, write numbers in the boxes to make a fraction that names one part.

Draw lines to divide the rectangle into 6 equal parts. Shade five parts. Then, write numbers in the boxes to make a fraction that names five parts.

Draw lines to divide the circle into 3 equal parts. Shade two parts. Then, write numbers in the boxes to make a fraction that names two parts.

Draw lines to divide the circle into 8 equal parts. Shade three parts. Then, write numbers in the boxes to make a fraction that names three parts.

FANTASTIC FRACTIONS!

Circle the fraction in each pair that is larger. The first one is done for you.

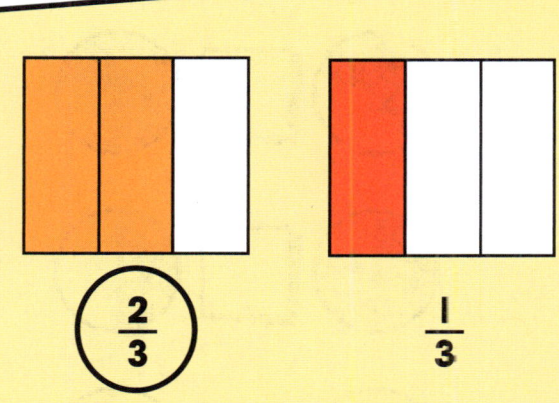

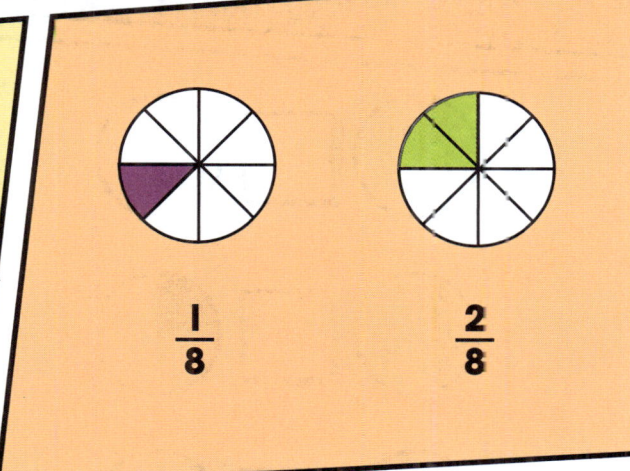

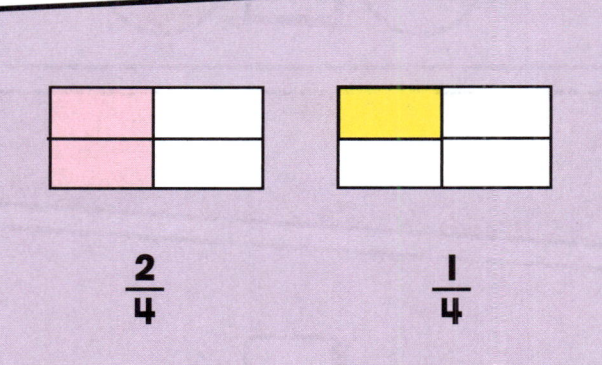

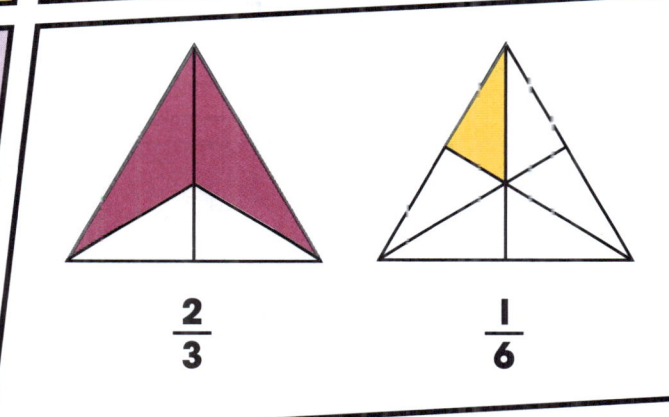

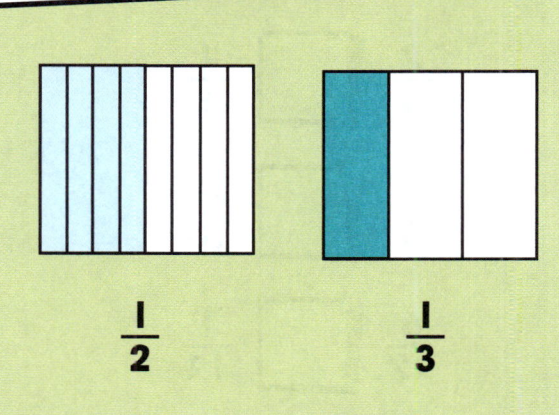

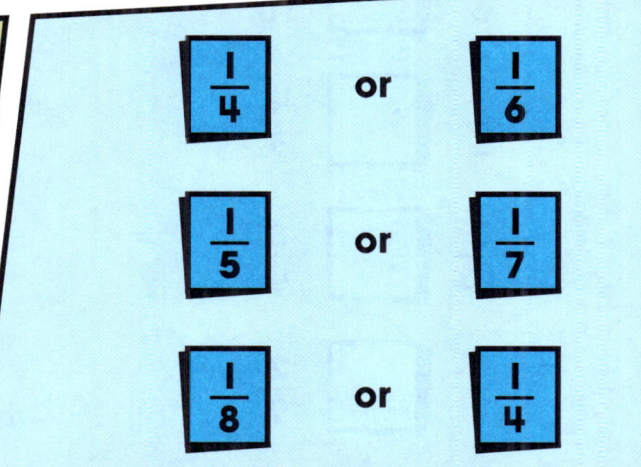

SUPER SKILL POWERS • GRADE 3   65

NAME _____

FANTASTIC FRACTIONS!

Compare the fractions shown by the colored areas in each pair of circles. Use the greater than (>), less than (<), or equal to (=) symbols.

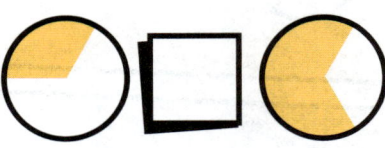

Compare the fractions. Use the greater than (>), less than (<), or equal to (=) symbols.

$\frac{1}{6}$ ☐ $\frac{1}{10}$ $\frac{2}{4}$ ☐ $\frac{2}{8}$

$\frac{3}{5}$ ☐ $\frac{4}{5}$ $\frac{2}{6}$ ☐ $\frac{4}{6}$

$\frac{3}{10}$ ☐ $\frac{3}{4}$ $\frac{4}{5}$ ☐ $\frac{4}{10}$

$\frac{5}{9}$ ☐ $\frac{2}{9}$ $\frac{6}{12}$ ☐ $\frac{1}{12}$

SUPER SKILL POWERS • GRADE 3

NAME _____

FANTASTIC FRACTIONS!

Mark each fraction on the number line.

$\frac{3}{4}$
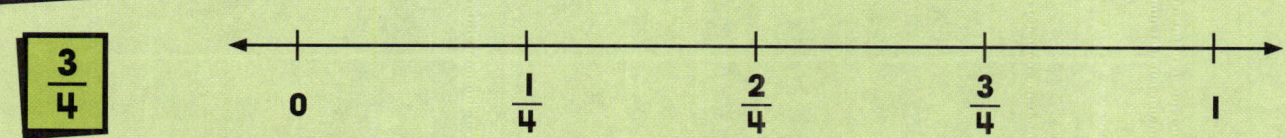

$\frac{5}{8}$
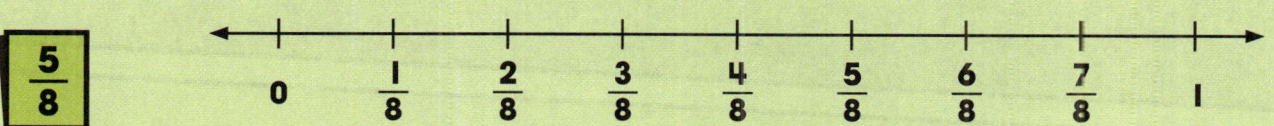

$\frac{10}{10}$ or 1 whole
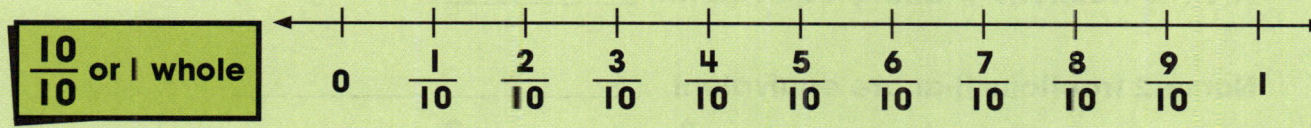

Shade the models to represent each fraction. If the fractions are equal, write = in the box. If they are not equal, write ≠.

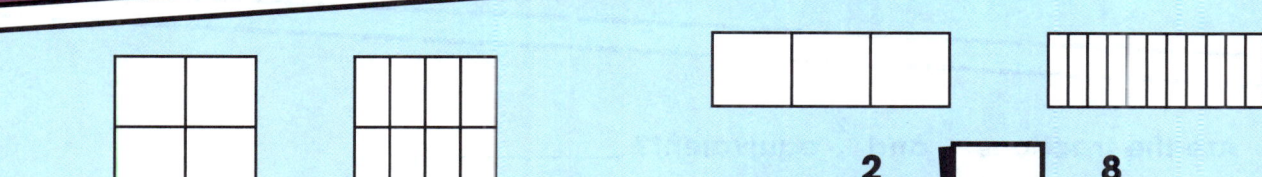

FANTASTIC FRACTIONS!

The fractions $\frac{2}{4}$ and $\frac{1}{2}$ are equivalent because they are at the same spot on the number line.

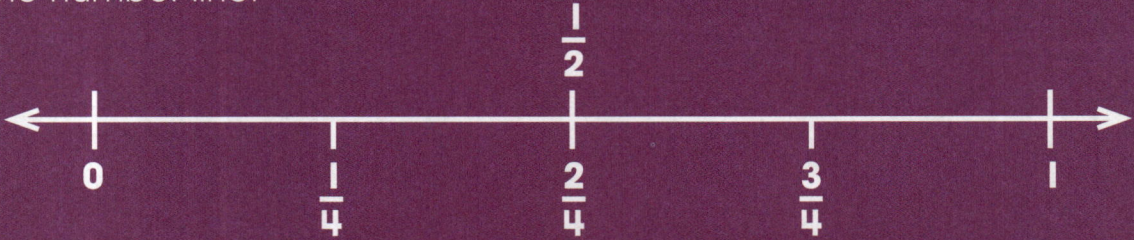

Answer the questions based on the number lines.

Are the fractions $\frac{1}{8}$ and $\frac{1}{4}$ equivalent? _____

Name 2 fractions that are equivalent. _____ _____

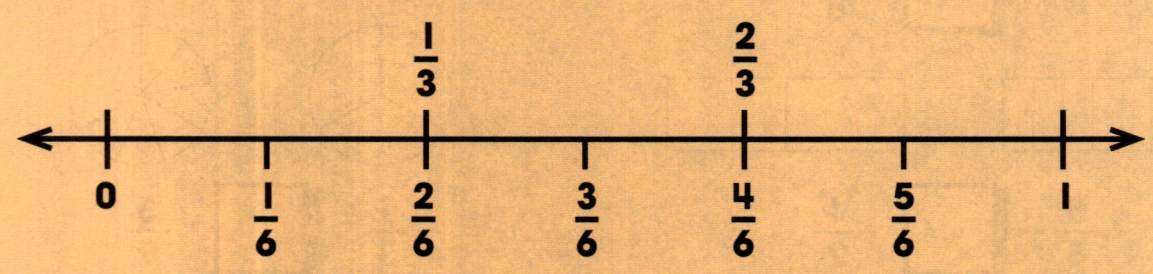

Are the fractions $\frac{1}{6}$ and $\frac{2}{3}$ equivalent? _____

Name 2 fractions that are equivalent. _____ _____

NAME _____

FANTASTIC FRACTIONS!

Draw a line to match the shapes in each group that show the same fraction shaded.

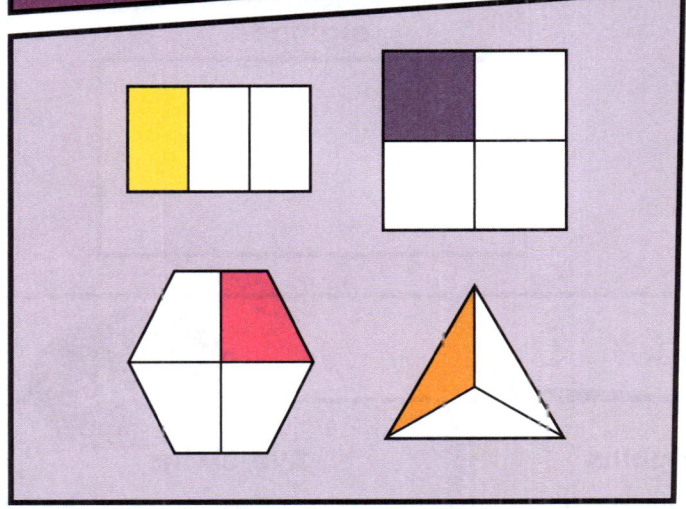 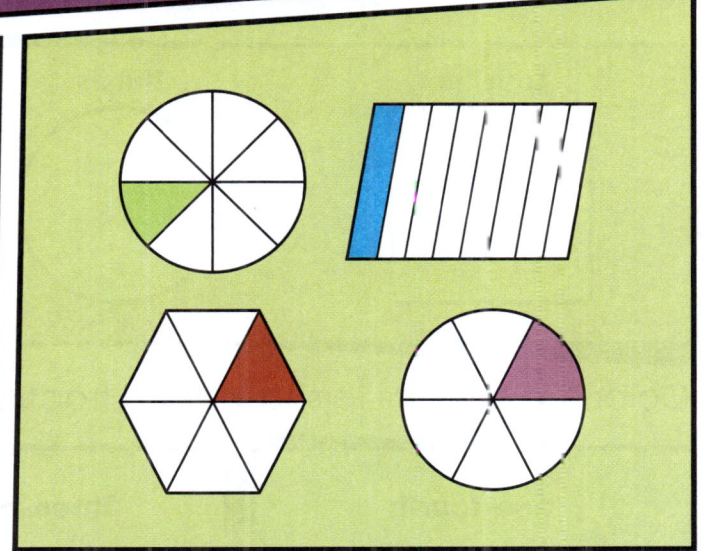

Draw a line between fractions that are equivalent, or equal.

$\frac{1}{2}$ 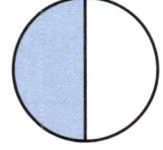	$\frac{3}{9}$ 
$\frac{4}{6}$ 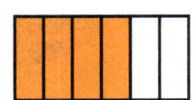	$\frac{2}{4}$ 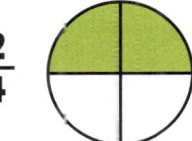
$\frac{4}{4}$ 	$\frac{2}{3}$ 
$\frac{1}{3}$ 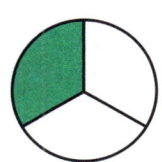	$\frac{1}{1}$ 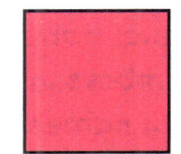

SUPER SKILL POWERS • GRADE 3   **69**

NAME _____

ASSESSMENT: FRACTIONS

Draw lines to divide each shape according to the fraction given.

3 pts

| fourths | thirds | eighths |

Color the objects to show each fraction.

3 pts

one-fourth   three-eighths    five-sixths

Follow the directions.

2 pts

Draw lines to divide the circle into 8 equal parts. Shade five parts. Then, write numbers in the boxes to make a fraction that names five parts.

Draw lines to divide the square into 6 equal parts. Shade four parts. Then, write numbers in the boxes to make a fraction that names four parts.

70 SUPER SKILL POWERS • GRADE 3

NAME _____

ASSESSMENT: FRACTIONS

Use >, <, or = to compare the fractions. **3 pts**

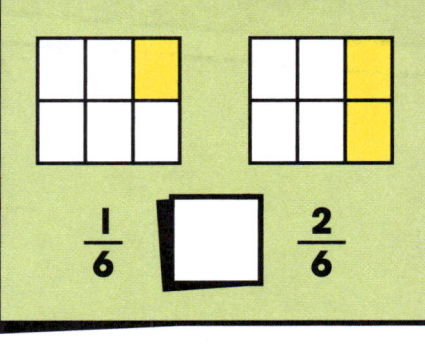
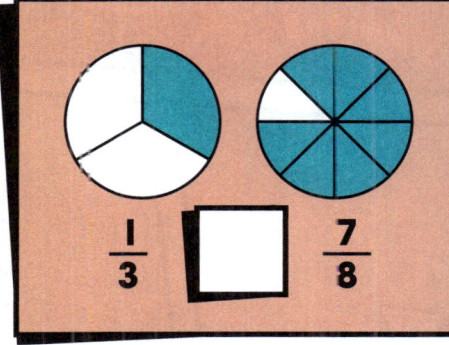
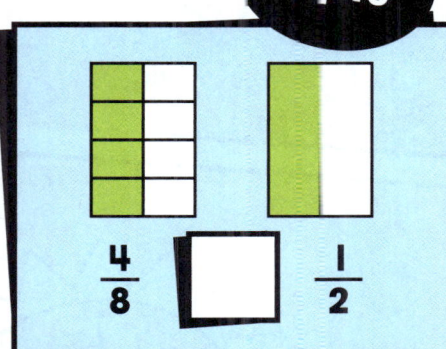

What fraction of each figure is shaded? Use >, <, or = to compare the fractions. **3 pts**

Label the fractions on the number line. Then, answer the question. **2 pts**

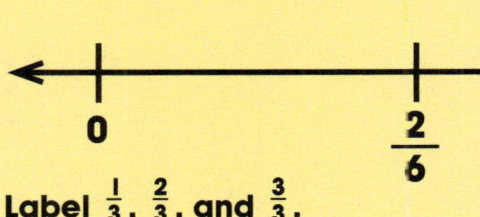

Label $\frac{1}{3}$, $\frac{2}{3}$, and $\frac{3}{3}$.

Are the fractions $\frac{2}{3}$ and $\frac{4}{6}$ equivalent? _____

YOUR SCORE ___ / 16

13–16 CORRECT ANSWERS = 1 STICKER

BONUS FRACTIONS!

Practice dividing real-world shapes into fractions. Draw shapes you see in the neighborhood or town. Divide the shape into 2, 3, 4, 6, or 8 parts. Then, shade one or more of the parts to show a fraction. Finally, write the fraction in fraction form.

NAME _____

BONUS FRACTIONS!

SUPER SKILL POWERS • GRADE 3

NAME _____

BONUS FRACTIONS!

NAME _____

MAGNIFICENT MEASUREMENT!

Count the square units in each figure to find the area. The first one is done for you.

4 m
3 m
A = __12__ sq. m

2 cm
5 cm
A = _____ sq. cm

3 in.
8 in.
A = _____ sq. in.

7 m
4 m
A = _____ sq. m

7 cm
1 cm
A = _____ sq. cm

4 in.
3 in.
A = _____ sq. in.

MAGNIFICENT MEASUREMENT!

Draw the square units to find the area. The first one is done for you.

3 in.
6 in.

A = __18__ sq. in.

4 cm
7 cm

A = _____ sq. cm

3 in.
3 in.

A = _____ sq. in.

3 m
1 m

A = _____ sq. m

2 cm
2 cm

A = _____ sq. cm

1 cm
5 cm

A = _____ sq. cm

MAGNIFICENT MEASUREMENT!

To find the area of a square or rectangle, multiply length by width. Find the area of each shape below. The first one is done for you.

15 in. / **5 in.** — <u>75</u> sq. in.

10 ft. / **4 ft.** — ____ sq. ft.

8 ft. / **7 ft.** — ____ sq. ft.

5 in. / **8 in.** — ____ sq. in.

7 yd. / **25 yd.** — ____ sq. yd.

8 yd. / **20 yd.** — ____ sq. yd.

78 SUPER SKILL POWERS • GRADE 3

NAME _____

MAGNIFICENT MEASUREMENT!

Draw the square units to find the area of each rectangle. Then, multiply to check your answer.

2 in.
2 in.

____ × ____ = ____

A = _____ sq. in.

3 cm
8 cm

____ × ____ = ____

A = _____ sq. cm

Write a multiplication problem to find the area of each rectangle.

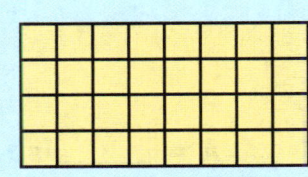

Area = ____ × ____ = ____ square units

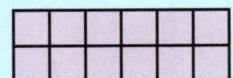

Area = ____ × ____ = ____ square units

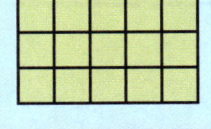

Area = ____ × ____ = ____ square units

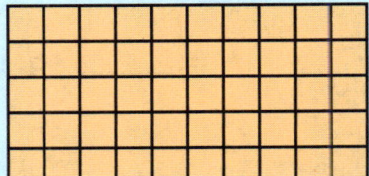

Area = ____ × ____ = ____ square units

NAME _____

MAGNIFICENT MEASUREMENT!

Find the area of each shape. The first one is done for you.

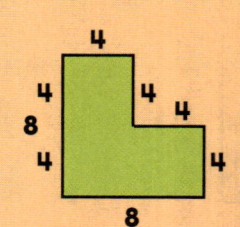

A = __16__ sq. units

A = __32__ sq. units

A = __48__ sq. units

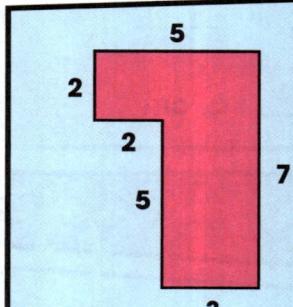

A = _____ sq. units

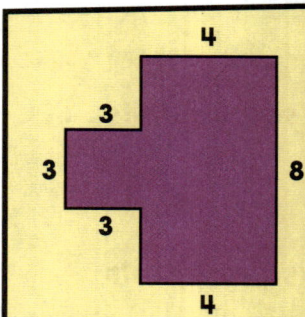

A = _____ sq. units

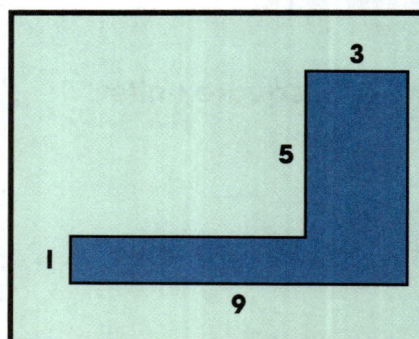

A = _____ sq. units

MAGNIFICENT MEASUREMENT!

Find the area of each shape.

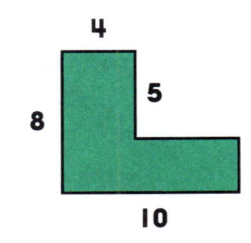

A = _____ sq. units

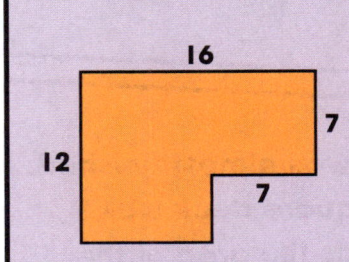

A = _____ sq. units

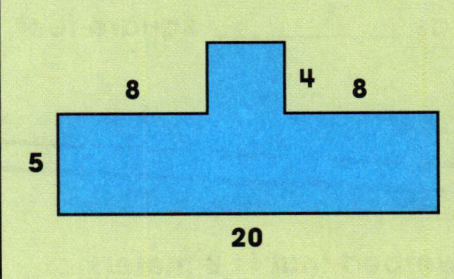

A = _____ sq. units

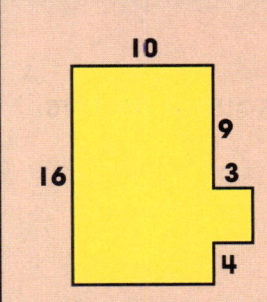

A = _____ sq. units

SUPER SKILL POWERS • GRADE 3

MAGNIFICENT MEASUREMENT!

Solve.

The Garcia brothers are painting a wall in their living room. The wall measures 8 feet by 10 feet. What is the area of the wall?

The area of the wall is _____ square feet.

Freda is putting carpet down in a room that measures 9 feet long by 10 feet wide. What is the area of the room?

The area is _____ square feet.

The zoo is building a new hippo pool that will measure 50 feet by 9 feet. What is the area of the pool?

The area is _____ square feet.

The Foster's deck was almost finished. Each side of the square deck was 9 feet long. What was the area of the deck?

The area was _____ square feet.

The college donated land for a park. The land is 90 feet long and 9 feet wide. What is the area of the land?

The area is _____ square feet.

Jill digs a flowerbed that is 8 meters long and 7 meters wide. What is the area of the flowerbed?

The area is _____ square meters.

NAME _____

MAGNIFICENT MEASUREMENT!

Perimeter is the distance all the way around a shape. Write the perimeter of each figure.

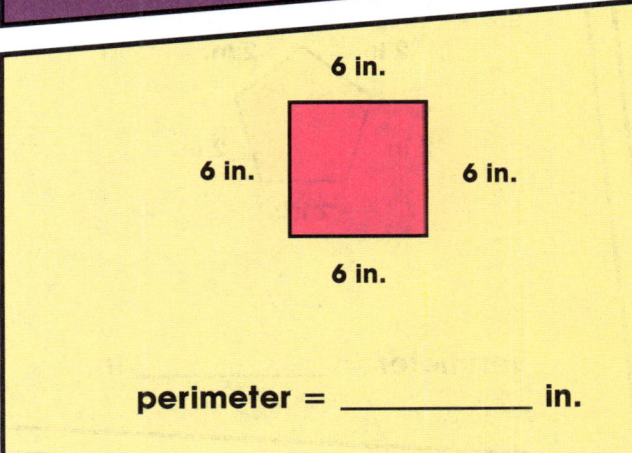

perimeter = _____ in.

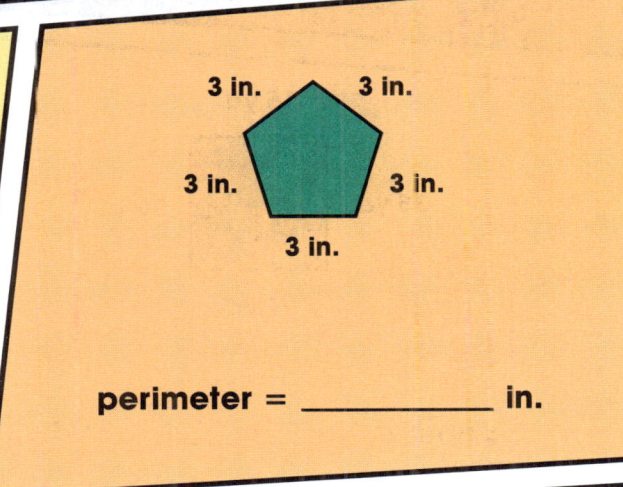

perimeter = _____ in.

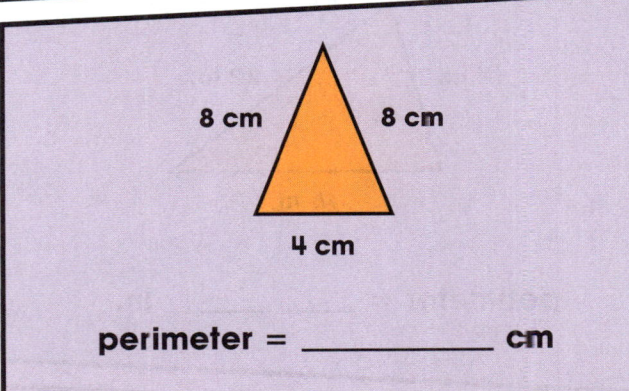

perimeter = _____ cm

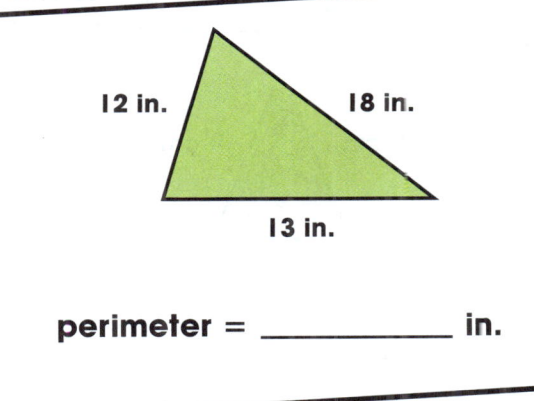

perimeter = _____ in.

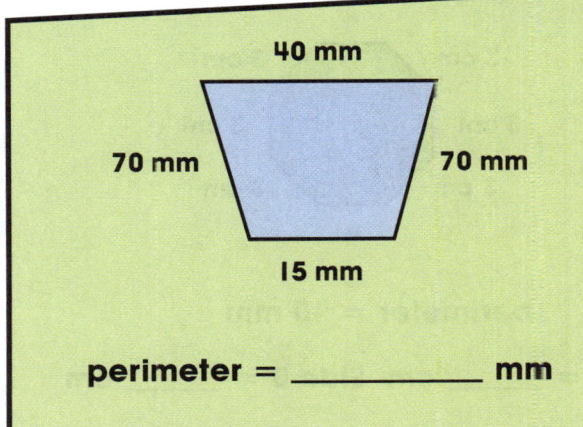

perimeter = _____ mm

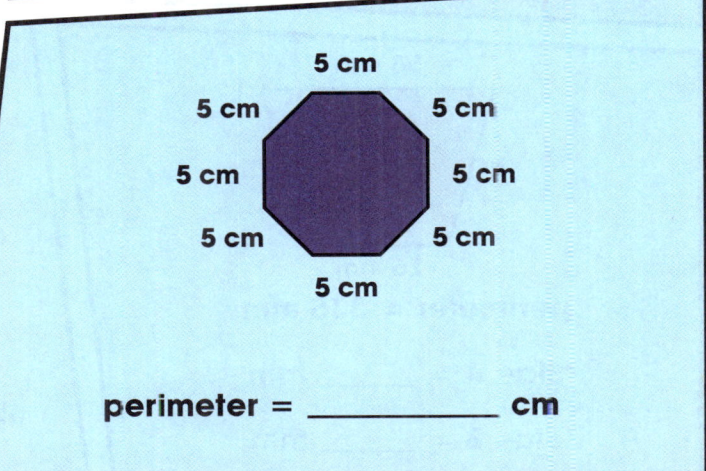

perimeter = _____ cm

NAME _____

MAGNIFICENT MEASUREMENT!

Write the perimeter of each figure or the missing side lengths.

35 yd.

35 yd.   35 yd.

35 yd.

perimeter = _____ yd.

2 in.   2 in.

2 in.   2 in.

2 in.

perimeter = _____ in.

4 cm   4 cm

3 cm

perimeter = _____ cm

14 in.   22 in.

15 in.

perimeter = _____ in.

50 mm

A   B

25 mm

perimeter = 235 mm

Side A = _____ mm

Side B = _____ mm

A

3 cm   3 cm

3 cm   3 cm

3 cm   3 cm

B

perimeter = 40 mm

Side A = _____ cm   Side B = _____ cm

84 SUPER SKILL POWERS • GRADE 3

MAGNIFICENT MEASUREMENT!

Solve.

The town of Yarmouth is planning a skateboard park and needs to know the perimeter of the park. The property measures 7 yards by 3 yards by 10 yards by 5 yards. What is the perimeter?

The park's perimeter is _____ yards.

John cleared a vacant lot to plant a garden. The rectangular lot measured 35 by 15 feet. What is the perimeter of the garden lot?

The perimeter of the lot is _____ feet.

Gabriel built a cage for his tropical birds. The cage is 14 feet long and 12 feet wide. What is the perimeter of the cage?

The perimeter of the cage is _____ feet.

The length of the playground is 103 feet, and the width is 50 feet. What is the perimeter of the playground?

The perimeter is _____ feet.

Anna is buying trim to go around her rug. Her rectangular rug measures 54 inches by 42 inches. How many inches of trim will Anna need to buy?

Anna will need to buy _____ inches of trim.

Natalie is putting a fence around her pool. Her pool is 10 feet long and 8 feet wide. How many feet of fencing will Natalie need?

Natalie will need _____ feet of fencing.

SUPER SKILL POWERS • GRADE 3   85

NAME _____

ASSESSMENT: MEASUREMENT

Find the area of the figure.

2 pts

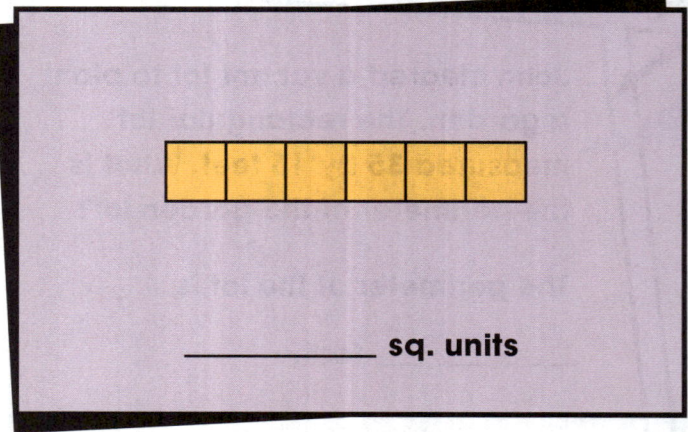

_____ sq. units

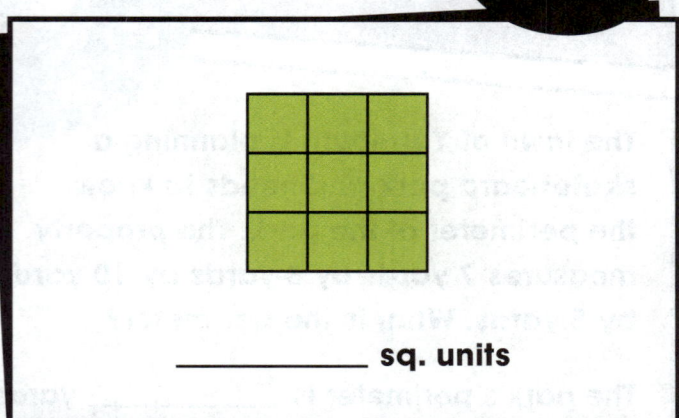

_____ sq. units

Follow the directions to solve each problem.

4 pts

Draw the square units to show the area of the rectangle.

```
        8
    ┌───────┐
  3 │       │ 3
    └───────┘
        8
```

A = _____ sq. units

Multiply to find the area.

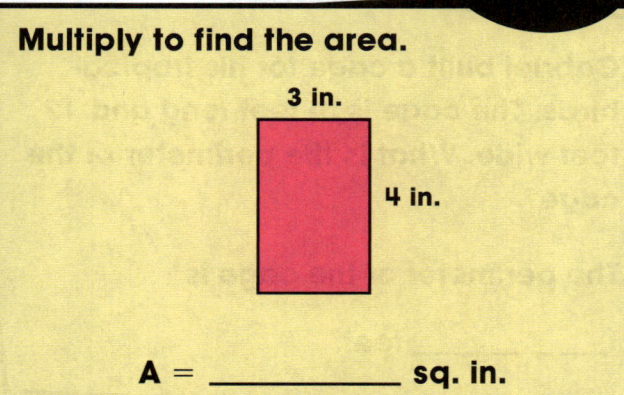

A = _____ sq. in.

Find the area.

```
      3
    ┌───┐
    │   │ 3
  6 │   └─────┐
    │         │ 3
    └─────────┘
         8
```

A = _____ sq. units

Solve.

An equilateral triangle has one side that measures 9 cm. How many centimeters is the perimeter of the triangle?

_____

86 SUPER SKILL POWERS • GRADE 3

NAME _____

ASSESSMENT: MEASUREMENT

Find the perimeter of each shape.   **4 pts**

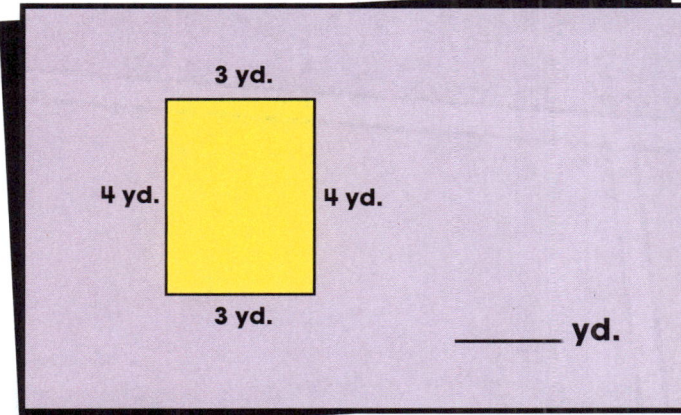

_____ yd.

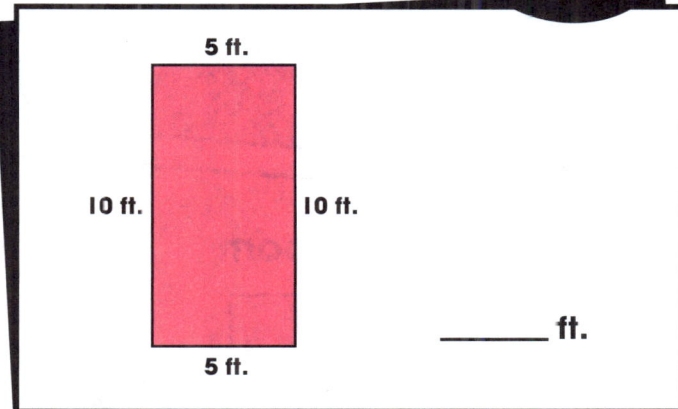

_____ ft.

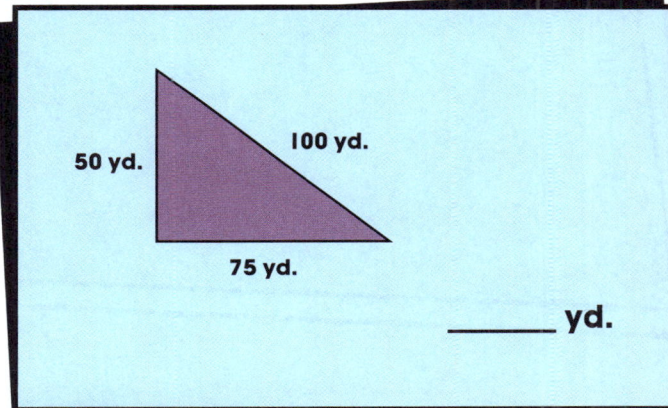

_____ yd.

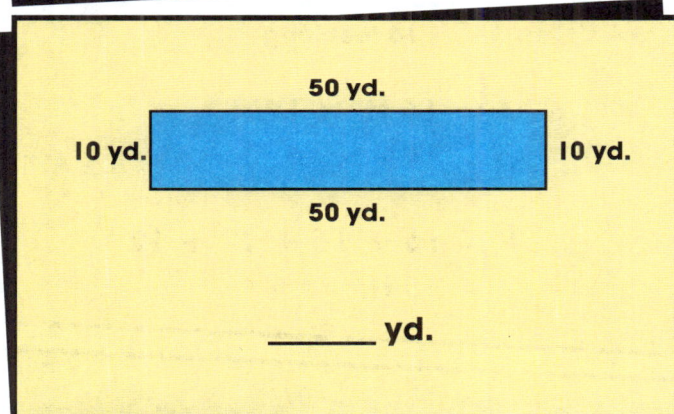

_____ yd.

Solve each problem.   **2 pts**

The rectangular third-grade classroom has a perimeter of 130 feet. If it is 25 feet wide, how many feet long is the classroom?

The classroom is _____ feet long.

Emma wants to tile her kitchen floor. How many 1-foot square tiles will she need if her floor is 10 feet long by 9 feet wide?

Emma will need _____ tiles.

YOUR SCORE ___ / 12

10–12 CORRECT ANSWERS = 1 STICKER

NAME _____

BONUS MEASUREMENT!

Practice finding area and perimeter. Using a tape measure or yard stick, measure rooms in your home, squares of sidewalk, and other rectangular items. In each comic strip frame, name an item and write down its measurements. Then, write one equation to find the area and another to find the perimeter, and solve.

Living Room

12 feet wide

16 feet long

A = 16 ft. × 12 ft.
A = 192 sq. ft.

P = 16 + 16 + 12 + 12
P = 56 ft.

NAME _____

BONUS MEASUREMENT!

NAME _____

BONUS MEASUREMENT!

NAME _____

SUPER TIME!

Complete the following. The first one is done for you.

6:15 means __15__ minutes after __6__.   6:15 means ____ minutes to ____.

7:50 means ____ minutes after ____.   7:50 means ____ minutes to ____.

12:45 means ____ minutes after ____.   12:45 means ____ minutes to ____.

1:30 means ____ minutes after ____.   1:30 means ____ minutes to ____.

Write the numerals shown on each clock.

___ : ___   ___ : ___   ___ : ___   ___ : ___

___ : ___   ___ : ___   ___ : ___   ___ : ___

SUPER TIME!

Write the time to the nearest hour, half hour, quarter hour, or minute as indicated.

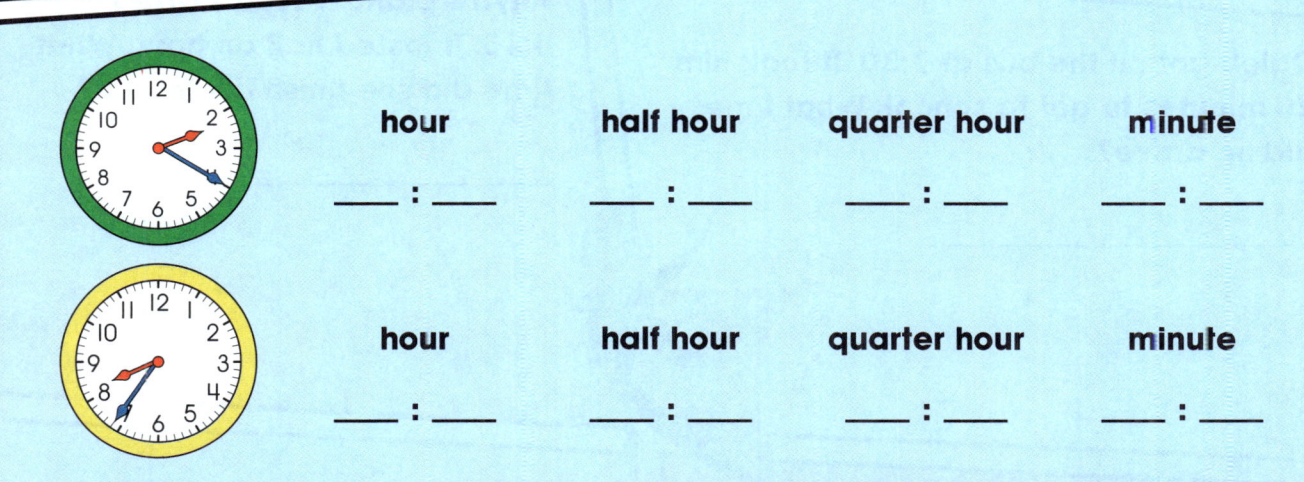

hour	half hour	quarter hour	minute
___ : ___	___ : ___	___ : ___	___ : ___

hour	half hour	quarter hour	minute
___ : ___	___ : ___	___ : ___	___ : ___

Draw the hands on the analog clock to match the time shown on each digital clock.

NAME _____

SUPER TIME!

Solve the word problems about time.

Caleb got on the bus at 7:30. It took him 20 minutes to get to school. What time did he arrive?

_____

Aliya's piano lesson started at 4:15. It lasted half an hour. What time did she finish her lesson?

_____

It started raining at 6:05. It rained for 45 minutes. What time did it stop raining?

_____

Mr. Domingo's class got to the museum at 9:00. They left two and one-half hours later. What time did they leave?

_____

Captain Quotient left Super Squad headquarters at 7:20. It took him 30 minutes to solve some tricky division problems and then return to headquarters. What time did he get back?

_____

The Red Writer started a letter to the mayor at 3:05. It took her 45 minutes to finish the letter and drop it off at the post office. What time was it when she mailed her letter?

_____

SUPER TIME!

Write the time shown on each clock.

Draw hands on each clock to show the correct time.

NAME _____

SUPER TIME!

Write the time shown on each clock.

Draw hands on each clock to show the correct time.

NAME _____

SUPER TIME!

Write the time shown on each clock.

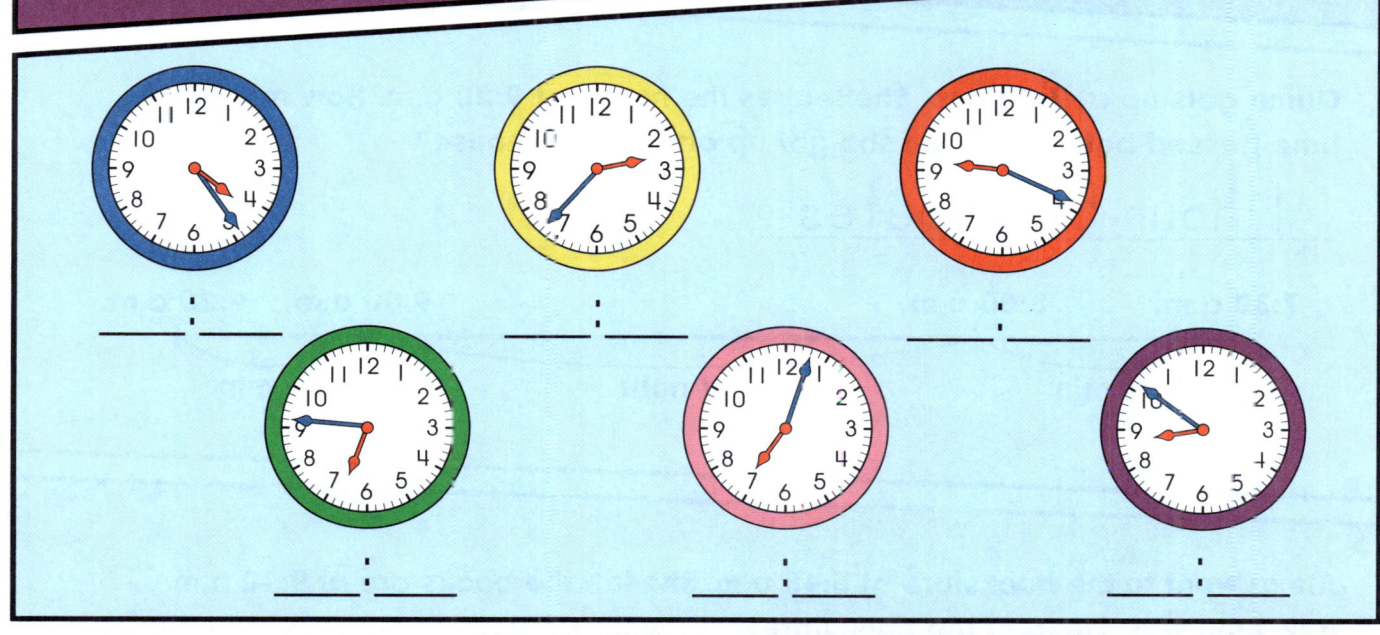

Draw hands on each clock to show the correct time.

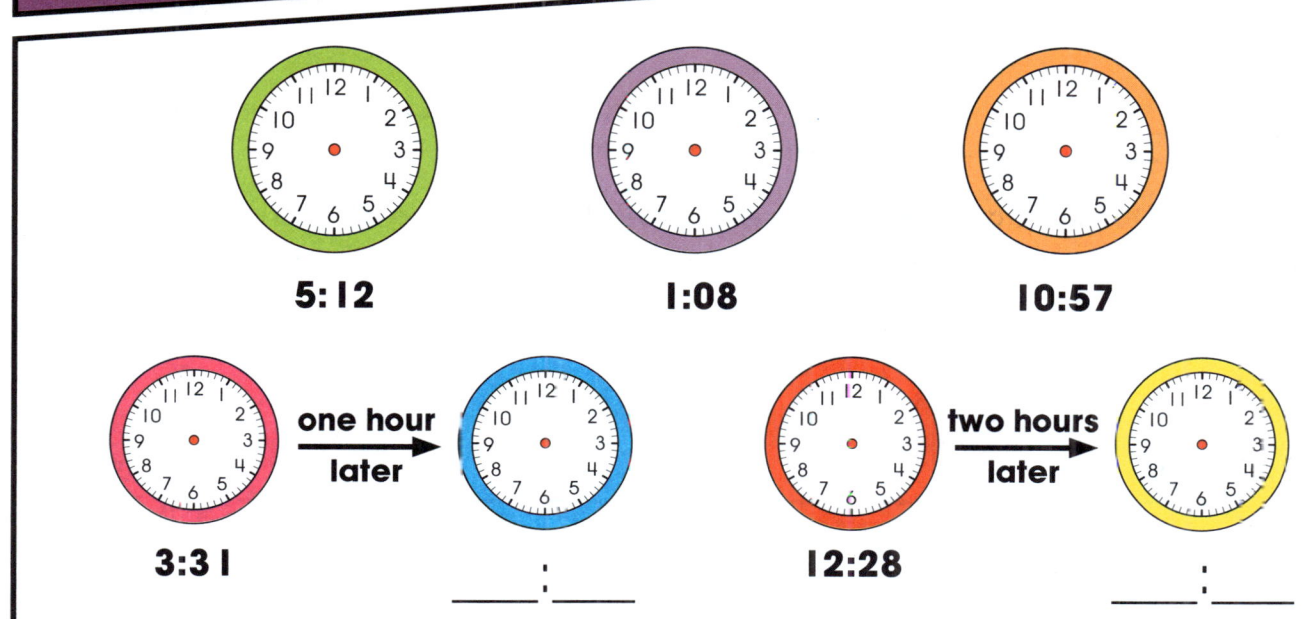

5:12   1:08   10:57

3:31 one hour later   12:28 two hours later

SUPER SKILL POWERS • GRADE 1

NAME _____

SUPER TIME!

Use the number line to solve each problem. The first one is done for you.

Quinn gets up at 7:30 a.m. She leaves the house at 9:20 a.m. How much time passed between when she got up and left the house?

1 hour 50 minutes

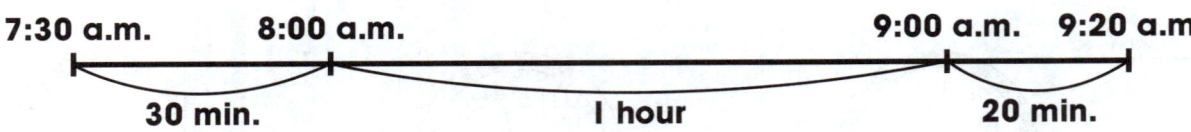

7:30 a.m. 8:00 a.m. 9:00 a.m. 9:20 a.m.
  30 min.   1 hour   20 min.

Alexa went to the bookstore at 5:45 p.m. She left the bookstore at 9:10 p.m. How long was Alexa at the bookstore?

_____

5:45 p.m. ———————————————— 9:10 p.m.

Hugo leaves for work at 7:45 a.m. He leaves work to go home at 4:15 p.m. How much time does Hugo spend at work?

_____

7:45 a.m. ———————————————— 4:15 p.m.

98 SUPER SKILL POWERS • GRADE 3

NAME _____

SUPER TIME!

Solve. Show the elapsed time on the number line. (Remember, 1 hour equals 60 minutes.)

Fiona takes her puppy to the park at 8:40 a.m. She goes to the lake, then to a friend's house, and gets home at 12:10 p.m. How much time was Fiona out of the house?

_____

8:40 a.m. ──────────────────────────── 12:10 p.m.

Jonathan goes to school at 8:50 a.m. The last bell rings at 3:05 p.m. How much time is Jonathan at school?

_____

8:50 a.m. ──────────────────────────── 3:05 p.m.

Graham went to sleep at 9:10 p.m. His alarm woke him up for school at 6:45 a.m. How long was Graham asleep?

_____

9:10 p.m. ──────────────────────────── 6:45 a.m.

Fernando and his family went to an amusement park on Saturday. They arrived at 10:30 a.m. and left for home at 9:50 p.m. How long were they at the park?

_____

10:30 a.m. ──────────────────────────── 9:50 p.m.

SUPER SKILL POWERS • GRADE 3   **99**

SUPER TIME!

Add the hours and minutes together. (Remember, 1 hour equals 60 minutes.) The first one is done for you.

```
   2 hours   10 minutes          4 hours   20 minutes
+  1 hour    50 minutes       +  2 hours   10 minutes
   ─────────────────             ─────────────────
   3 hours   60 minutes
   or 4 hours
```

```
   9 hours              1 hour               6 hours
+  2 hours           +  5 hours           +  3 hours
   ────────             ────────             ────────
```

```
   6 hours   15 minutes      10 hours  30 minutes      3 hours   40 minutes
+  1 hour    15 minutes    +  1 hour   10 minutes    + 8 hours   20 minutes
   ─────────────────          ─────────────────         ─────────────────
```

```
  11 hours  15 minutes       4 hours   15 minutes      7 hours   10 minutes
+  1 hour   30 minutes    +  5 hours   45 minutes    + 1 hour    30 minutes
   ─────────────────          ─────────────────         ─────────────────
```

SUPER TIME!

Subtract the hours and minutes. (Remember, 1 hour equals 60 minutes.) The first one is done for you

    5   70
  ~~6~~ hours ~~10~~ minutes
− 2 hour   30 minutes
───────────────────
  3 hours 40 minutes

4 hours 20 minutes
− 2 hours 10 minutes
───────────────────

12 hours
− 2 hours
────────

5 hours
− 3 hours
────────

2 hours
− 1 hour
────────

5 hours 30 minutes
− 2 hours 15 minutes
───────────────────

9 hours 45 minutes
− 3 hours 15 minutes
───────────────────

11 hours 50 minutes
− 4 hours 35 minutes
───────────────────

12 hours
− 6 hours 30 minutes
───────────────────

7 hours 15 minutes
− 5 hours 30 minutes
───────────────────

8 hours 10 minutes
− 4 hours 40 minutes
───────────────────

NAME _____

ASSESSMENT: TIME

Complete the following. **4 pts**

2:32 means _____ minutes after _____.   2:32 means _____ minutes to _____.

3:45 means _____ minutes after _____.   3:45 means _____ minutes to _____.

Tell the time to the nearest hour, half hour, quarter hour, or minute as indicated. **4 pts**

hour	half hour	quarter hour	minute
___ : ___	___ : ___	___ : ___	___ : ___

Solve the word problems about time. **2 pts**

Carrie's family leaves at 7:15 a.m. They drive for 30 minutes and then stop for dinner. What time is it when they stop?

_____

Look at the clock. Blair arrived at the bus stop 45 minutes ago. What time did Blair arrive at the bus stop?

_____

Solve the problem. Use the number line to show how much time has elapsed. **2 pts**

Blane left work at 2:15 p.m. He ate dinner at 7:15 p.m. How much time passed between the time Blane left work and ate dinner?

2:15 p.m. ⊢—————————————⊣ 7:15 p.m.

_____

YOUR SCORE

12

10–12 CORRECT ANSWERS = 1 STICKER

SUPER SKILL POWERS • GRADE 3

BONUS TIME!

Practice telling time on real clocks. A couple times a day, read the time on a digital or analog clock. Write the current time in a comic strip frame, and then draw the time on the analog clock provided.

 4:07

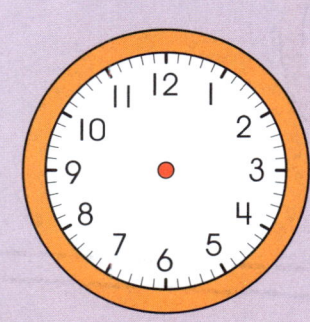

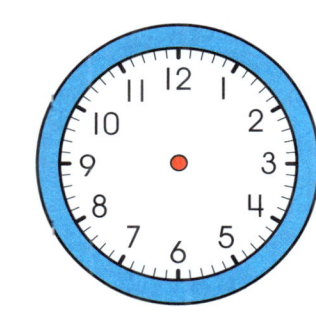

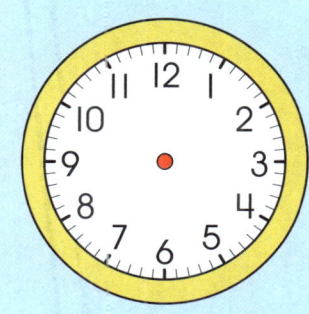

NAME _____

BONUS TIME!

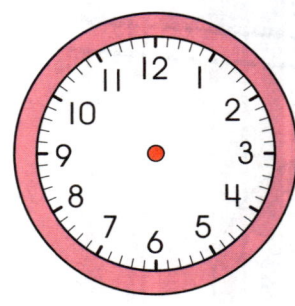

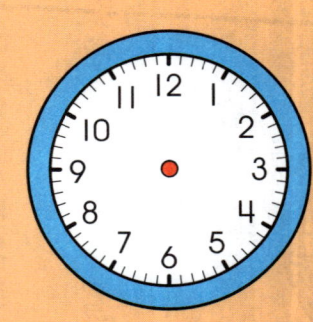

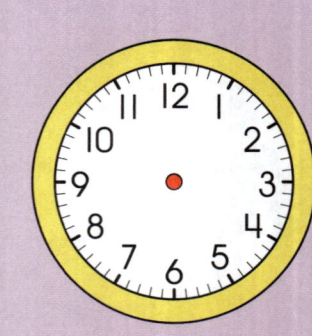

NAME _____

BONUS TIME!

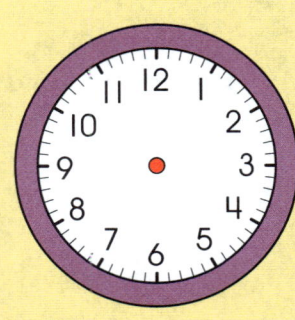

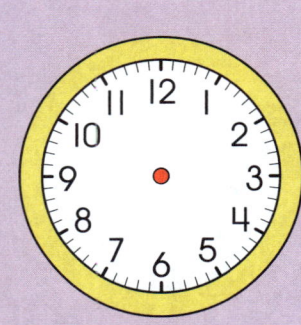
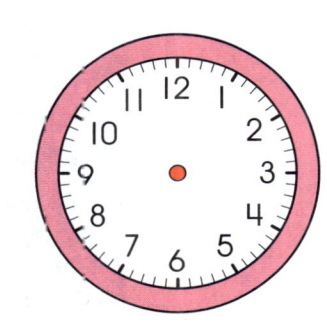

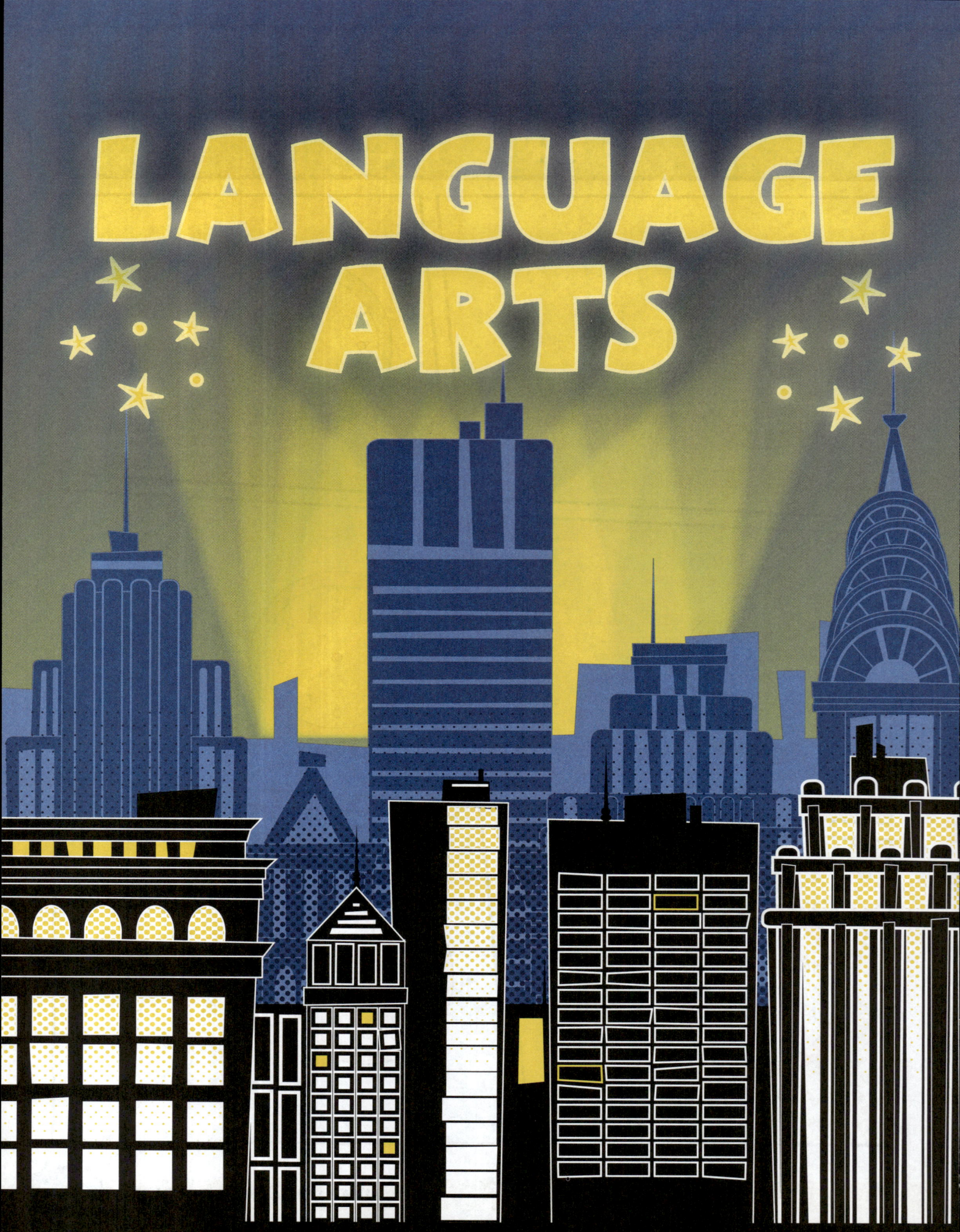

NAME _____

PHENOMENAL NOUNS AND VERBS!

Abstract nouns are feelings, concepts, and ideas. Some examples are **hope**, **bravery**, and **pride**. Underline the abstract noun in each sentence.

Colonel Graham knows that the cadets have respect for him.

We were so grateful for our neighbors' generosity after the fire.

"I am almost out of patience," warned Mom.

We could see Izzy's satisfaction when she finally finished the puzzle.

Ryan's silliness made the whole group laugh.

Complete each sentence with an abstract noun from the box.

| hope | beauty | courage | talent | sympathy |

Dionne showed _____ when she faced the auditorium and started to speak.

I felt _____ for the poor bird with the broken wing.

The _____ of the forest was truly awesome.

Carolina had _____ that everything would turn out well.

My brother has a _____ for making the whole family laugh.

NAME _____

PHENOMENAL NOUNS AND VERBS!

Underline the abstract noun in each sentence.

Mr. and Mrs. Ito were filled with pride when Jessica won the spelling bee.

Mom always talks about the wonderful childhood she had with her sisters.

My favorite thing about Jorge is his kindness.

Cole could see the delight on Lea's face as she opened her gift.

"I really appreciate your honesty," said Principal Jenkins.

I can count on Lindsay to always tell me the truth.

Write three sentences of your own, using the abstract nouns in the boxes.

honesty
_____
_____

beauty
_____
_____

patience
_____
_____

SUPER SKILL POWERS • GRADE 3

PHENOMENAL NOUNS AND VERBS!

Am, **is**, and **are** are all different forms of the verb **to be**. **Am** is used only with the subject **I**. **Is** is used when the subject is singular. **Are** is used with the subject **you**. **Are** is also used when the subject is plural. Rewrite each sentence below. If it has a plural subject, rewrite it with a single subject. If it has a single subject, rewrite it with a plural subject.
The first one is done for you.

The salad dressing and the salad are on the table.

The salad dressing is on the table.

Nissa and Toby are eight.

_____

The photograph is in an album.

_____

The CDs on the shelf are from the library.

_____

We are excited about traveling to Mexico.

_____

PHENOMENAL NOUNS AND VERBS!

Read the paragraphs. There are 11 mistakes with the verbs **am**, **is**, and **are**. Cross out each mistake. Then, write the correct form of the verb above it.

    A topiary (toe pee air ee) are a kind of sculpture made from plants. Topiaries is cut to look like many different things. Some am shaped like animals. For example, a topiary can look like an elephant, a bear, a horse, or even a dinosaur. Other topiaries is trimmed to look like castles, cones, or mazes.

    A topiary gardener are an artist. He or she can turn simple shrubs into beautiful sculptures. Boxwood, holly, bay laurel, and yew am some of the best plants to use for topiary. They is easy to train and to trim.

    In May, I are going to visit the Green Animals Topiary Garden in Rhode Island. It am one of the oldest topiary gardens in the country. There am 80 pieces of topiary there! It are fun to imagine all the green animals coming to life and roaming the gardens.

NAME _____

PHENOMENAL NOUNS AND VERBS!

Has and **have** are different forms of the verb **to have**. **Have** is used when the subject is **I** or **you**. **Have** is also used with plural subjects. **Has** is used when there is a single subject like **he**, **she**, or **it**. Complete each sentence below with the word **has** or **have**. Write the correct word on the line.

Gus and Emily _____ a shell collection.

A horse conch _____ a cone shape and can grow to be almost two feet long.

Shells _____ value when they are beautiful or rare.

The shapes of some shells _____ interesting names, like helmet, basket, lamp, frog, and trumpet.

Oysters and clams _____ shells that are hinged at the back.

Emily _____ a necklace made from polished pieces of shell.

Cowrie shells _____ been used as money on Indian and Pacific islands.

If Gus _____ more than one of a certain shell, he will trade it with other collectors.

PHENOMENAL NOUNS AND VERBS!

Read the letter. There are eight mistakes with the verbs **have** and **has**. Cross out each incorrect verb. Then, write the correct form of the verb above it.

August 6, 2016

Dear Kyra,

    How is life at home in Massachusetts? We are having a great time in Florida. Gus and I has 40 new shells to add to our collection! We has been busy searching the beaches here. Gus and I already has labels for our new shells. We don't want to forget their names by the time we get home.

    Some shells still has animals living in them. We never collect those shells. Our parents has helped us look in rock crevices and tide pools. That is how we found a true tulip shell. It have a pretty peachy color and an interesting pattern.

    I has a surprise to bring home for you. You has never seen a shell like this. I can't wait to see you. Wish you were here!

Your friend,

Emily

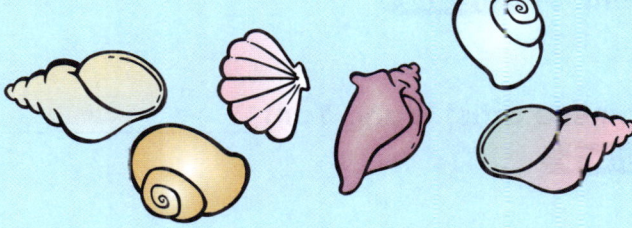

NAME _____

PHENOMENAL NOUNS AND VERBS!

Verbs in the **present tense** tell about things that are happening right now. Verbs in the **past tense** tell about things that have already happened. Add **ed** to a regular verb to change it to the past tense. If the verb already ends in **e**, just add **d**. If a verb ends in **y**, change the **y** to **i** and add **ed**. Read the sentences below. Complete each sentence with the past tense of the verb in the box.

Leonardo da Vinci _____ the mysterious Mona Lisa. **paint**

Women and children often _____ for artist Mary Cassatt. **pose**

The Impressionists _____ the world that not all paintings had to look realistic. **show**

Grandma Moses _____ to paint cheerful pictures of life in the country. **love**

Jackson Pollack, who made colorful paint-splattered paintings, _____ with Thomas Hart Benton. **study**

Vincent van Gogh _____ more than 800 oil paintings during his lifetime! **create**

Chinese artist Wang Yani _____ painting when she was only two. **start**

PHENOMENAL NOUNS AND VERBS!

Underline the verb in each sentence. Then, change it to the past tense and write the new verb on the line.

Norman Rockwell lives from 1894 until 1978.

_____

Norman studies at the National Academy of Design in New York.

_____

He illustrates issues of children's magazines, like *Boys' Life*.

_____

Norman paints scenes from everyday small town life.

_____

Norman calls himself a storyteller.

_____

A fire destroys many of Norman's paintings.

_____

Norman Rockwell receives the Presidential Medal of Freedom in 1976.

_____

NAME _____

PHENOMENAL NOUNS AND VERBS!

To form the past tense of some verbs, you must change the entire word. The verb **eat(s)** becomes **ate**; **say(s)** becomes **said**; **grow(s)** becomes **grew**; **make(s)** becomes **made**; and **ride(s)** becomes **rode**. In the paragraphs below, cross out the verbs in purple. Use this symbol (^), and write the past-tense verb above it.

When my mom was a little girl, her family owned a bakery. Mom says that she loved the sweet smell of bread and pastries baking in the ovens. Every morning, Mom eats a cinnamon roll for breakfast. She rides her bike to school when the weather was nice. In her bag, she carried fresh muffins for her teachers and her friends.

Each afternoon, she and her dad make crusty rolls and chewy bagels. Grandpa put all the ingredients in a big bowl. He and Mom took turns kneading the dough. Then, he covered it with a clean towel. The dough grows and grows. Mom says she loved to punch it down. Finally, she and Grandpa shaped the dough and popped it into the ovens. Mom's family eats fresh bread with dinner every night!

NAME _____

PHENOMENAL NOUNS AND VERBS!

Read each sentence below. On the line, write the past tense of the underlined verb.

Grandma always eats a blueberry bagel with cream cheese for breakfast.

_____

The Larsons say that Hot Cross Buns was the best bakery in town.

_____

Mom's cousin Eddie rides his bike around town and delivered bread.

_____

Mom grows up helping her parents at the bakery. _____

Every Saturday, Mom and Grandpa make 12 loaves of wheat bread, 15 loaves of French bread, and 100 dinner rolls. _____

Now, find each past-tense verb in the word search puzzle. Circle the words you find. Words are written across and down.

h	q	s	a	i	d	r
m	p	n	t	m	a	l
z	g	r	e	w	g	k
u	d	k	y	f	l	g
j	h	v	r	u	a	e
i	b	b	o	w	d	y
t	m	a	d	e	x	c
j	s	f	e	p	p	e

SUPER SKILL POWERS • GRADE 3

NAME _____

ASSESSMENT: NOUNS AND VERBS

Underline the abstract noun in each sentence. **5 pts**

You need patience when you are learning to play chess.

Amelia had a hard time showing courage when her flashlight went out.

Warren has a talent for painting with watercolors.

My sister and I were full of pride when our puppy learned to roll over.

Ms. Stark was impressed by my honesty when I confessed to breaking her lamp.

Circle the verb that correctly completes each sentence. **5 pts**

The horses _____ afraid to walk through the gate.   am   is   are

My favorite cartoon character _____ Bugs Bunny.   am   is   are

Wendy _____ waiting for the timer to go off.   am   is   are

Mr. Szoke _____ an extremely large book on his desk.   has   have

My friends _____ a trampoline in their backyard.   has   have

ASSESSMENT: NOUNS AND VERBS

Complete each sentence with the past tense of the verb in the box.

5 pts

Ursula's parents _____ the fruit smoothies she made for them. `love`

I _____ two bowls of cereal for breakfast this morning. `eat`

Trent's little brother _____ three inches last month! `grows`

Marcella _____ her best friend every night before bed. `calls`

Nicholas _____ his bike to school yesterday. `rides`

Underline the verb in each sentence. Then, change it to the past tense and write the new verb on the line.

5 pts

Our class paints a picture of the fish in the school aquarium. _____

The chef at the Chinese restaurant makes amazing dumplings. _____

Dad's second cousin Julian says hello. _____

Elijah shows me a spotted toad from his garden. _____

Do you know who illustrates this picture book? _____

YOUR SCORE ___ / 20

16–20 CORRECT ANSWERS = 1 STICKER

NAME _____

BONUS NOUNS AND VERBS!

SUPER SKILL POWERS • GRADE 3   121

NAME _____

BONUS NOUNS AND VERBS!

UNBELIEVABLE AGREEMENT!

Singular subjects take singular verbs. Singular verbs usually end with **s** or **es**. Plural subjects take plural verbs. Plural verbs do not have an added **s** or **es**. Read the paragraph below. Underline the subjects. Find the verbs that do not agree with their subjects, and cross them out. Then, write the correct verb above each. The first one is done for you.

          washes
Mr. Ruskin ~~wash~~ his historic car on Saturdays. Aaron and Ali helps him.

Mr. Ruskin sprays the old car with warm water. He scrub every inch of the car

with a big sponge. The children polishes the windshield and the mirrors.

They use clean, soft rags. Aaron wax the beautiful red car. It shine in the sunlight.

He wishes to have a car just like his dad's one day. Mr. Ruskin take Aaron and Ali

for a drive in the shiny car every Saturday afternoon. They buy ice-cream cones.

Then, they walks in the park.

NAME _____

UNBELIEVABLE AGREEMENT!

Circle the verb that correctly completes each sentence.

Emily and Mateo _____ a ball in the backyard. **toss, tosses**

The Jorgensons _____ their pumpkins every autumn.
harvest, harvests

My little brother _____ his teeth with an electric toothbrush.
brush, brushes

Britta _____ ten miles a day when she is in training for the race.
bike, bikes

The blender _____ the ingredients. **mix, mixes**

The Guzmans _____ near a crystal-clear mountain lake every summer.
camp, camps

Write a sentence using each given verb. Underline the subject in your sentence, and circle the verb. Make sure that the subject and the verb agree.

skate _____

watch _____

SUPER SKILL POWERS • GRADE 3   125

UNBELIEVABLE AGREEMENT!

The verbs **am**, **is**, and **are** and the verbs **has** and **have** are irregular. The form of the verb you use depends on the subject. Read each sentence below and circle the verb form that agrees with the subject. The first one is done for you.

I ((am) is are) on my way to school.

Ms. Caldero (am is are) a musician.

Do you (has have) the chicken pox?

You (am is are) the only one who understands.

The train (has have) a red caboose.

I (has have) a guinea pig named Moe.

The coins (am is are) in my piggy bank.

William and Dante (has have) blue bicycles.

I (am is are) so happy to see you!

Huskies (has have) thick fur and curly tails.

UNBELIEVABLE AGREEMENT!

Read the paragraphs. Cross out each incorrect verb. Then, write the correct form of the verb above it. You will find eight mistakes.

The Everglades cover about 4,000 square miles of land. They ~~is~~ located in southwestern Florida. Marshes and swamps ~~makes~~ up a large part of the Everglades. They are covered with saw grass. It ~~grow~~ to be about 15 feet tall. People cannot easily ~~reaches~~ much of the Everglades because the saw grass ~~am~~ so thick. This area ~~are~~ sometimes called *the river of grass*.

The Everglades have many different kinds of plants and wildlife. The tropical area makes a good home for birds like herons, egrets, spoonbills, and pelicans. The Everglades are the only place in the world that has both crocodiles and alligators. Deer, panthers, otters, and manatees ~~makes~~ their homes there, too. Quiet visitors ~~catches~~ a glimpse of many animals.

NAME _____

UNBELIEVABLE AGREEMENT!

Write the verb from the box that agrees with each subject.

| am | is | are |

Cara and I _____   Julian _____

The teachers _____   I _____

A rose _____   You _____

Underline the verb that completes each sentence.

Benji and Kate (**are, is**) going on a fall scavenger hunt.

Benji (**spot, spots**) a pumpkin on a neighbor's porch.

Kate (**sees, see**) a scarecrow.

Leaves (**dance, dances**) along the sidewalk as a breeze blows.

The oak tree at the end of the street (**drop, drops**) acorns on the ground.

Busy squirrels (**gather, gathers**) the nuts.

The children (**hear, hears**) the sound of geese calling overhead.

SUPER SKILL POWERS • GRADE 3

UNBELIEVABLE AGREEMENT!

A **pronoun** is a word that takes the place of a noun. Use subject pronouns like **I** and **we** when talking about the person or people doing the action. Use object pronouns like **me** and **us** when talking about the person or people the action is being done to. Read each sentence below. Write the correct pronoun in the blank. The first two are done for you.

___We___ are going to the picnic together.　　**We, Us**

They gave ___me___ the roller skates.　　**I, me**

_____ am finished with my science project.　　**me, I**

Eric passed the football to _____ .　　**me, I**

They ate dinner with _____ last night.　　**we, us**

_____ like spinach better than ice cream.　　**I, me**

Mom came in the room to tell _____ good night.　　**me, I**

_____ had a pizza party in our backyard.　　**Us, We**

They told _____ the good news.　　**us, we**

Tom and _____ went to the store.　　**me, I**

NAME _____

UNBELIEVABLE AGREEMENT!

Write the pronoun from the box that takes the place of each noun or noun pair in purple. The first one is done for you.

| he | she | it | they | him | her | them |

The **monkey** dropped the banana.   _It_

Dad washed the car last night.   _____

Mary and David took a walk in the park.   _____

Ellen spent the night at her grandmother's house.   _____

The baseball **players** lost their game.   _____

Mike Van Meter is a great soccer player.   _____

The **parrot** can say five different words.   _____

Megan wrote a story in class today.   _____

They gave a party for **Teresa**.   _____

Everyone in the class was happy for **Ethan**.   _____

The **children** petted the giraffe.   _____

UNBELIEVABLE AGREEMENT!

Circle the noun(s) or pronoun(s) that each underlined pronoun is replacing. The first one is done for you.

Betty has a (computer). She keeps it on her desk.

Liv forgot her umbrella. She went home to get it.

Perry and I forgot our backpacks, so we ran back home.

Benji asked Juan if he would teach him to hit a baseball.

Amira and Becca both collect seashells. Sometimes, they trade with each other.

Rachel plays the violin, and sometimes she sings, too.

The crayons were scattered on the floor. I had to pick them up.

We gave our dog a new toy. Fido barked when he saw it.

Our school bus is always crowded, and it is usually noisy, too.

I love pizza, but we only have it on Fridays.

NAME _____

UNBELIEVABLE AGREEMENT!

Write the pronoun that replaces each underlined noun. Some pronouns will be possessive. The first one is done for you.

Please tell <u>Garrett</u> that this piece of cake is for ____him____.

Jeff borrowed six <u>books</u> from the library, but he has lost one of _____.

At the fair, several <u>kids</u> lost _____ balloons.

Taj has three <u>frogs</u> as pets and loves _____ very much.

<u>Liam</u> remembered to brush _____ teeth before school.

The <u>hurricane</u> made landfall at 6:00, and _____ is headed this way!

Each <u>girl</u> gets an apple for _____ snack.

<u>Mom</u> asked about the fair, so I told _____ about Janelle's pig.

UNBELIEVABLE AGREEMENT!

Match the possessive pronouns with the words they replace.

Riley and I • • his

the book • • her

you • • our

Penny • • their

Simone and Spencer • • my

Robert • • your

I • • its

NAME _____

ASSESSMENT: AGREEMENT

Read each sentence. Using the present tense, write the form of the verb in the box that agrees with the subject. **5 pts**

Ivy and Gavin _____ to school when the weather is nice. **bike**

Erin's baby brother _____ her on the cheek. **kiss**

Edgar _____ his radio-controlled car whenever it breaks. **fix**

About 70 students _____ a cold at our school each November. **catch**

My best friend _____ on the next block. **live**

Write the verb from the box that correctly completes each sentence.   **am   are   has   have   is**   **5 pts**

The basketball _____ completely flat.

Turtles _____ hard shells and scaly skin.

You _____ amazingly good at spelling!

The mountain _____ evergreen trees on its surface.

I _____ not happy about my missing yo-yo.

ASSESSMENT: AGREEMENT

Write the pronoun that replaces each underlined noun. Some pronouns will be possessive.

5 pts

The <u>cows</u> left the barn, but _____ did not begin to graze.

<u>George</u> lost _____ pet spider on the bus.

I pushed the toy <u>sailboat</u>, and _____ floated across the pond.

<u>We</u> asked for cotton candy at the fair, but my mom got _____ apples.

<u>Erica</u> stubbed _____ toe on the coffee table.

Circle the noun(s) or pronoun(s) that each underlined pronoun is replacing.

5 pts

Jasper and I lost the house keys, so <u>we</u> waited on the porch for a half-hour.

The bird built <u>its</u> nest out of twigs and string.

I found six marbles on the floor, and I gave <u>them</u> to my teacher.

Amber stayed home because <u>she</u> was not feeling well.

Did you remember to bring <u>your</u> bathing suit

YOUR SCORE ____ / 20

16–20 CORRECT ANSWERS = 1 STICKER

NAME _____

BONUS AGREEMENT!

In each comic strip frame, name a person or group of people. Then, write a sentence that uses that name plus a pronoun that correctly replaces it. Underline the pronoun.

_____**Mom**_____

Mom closed the car door with <u>her</u> foot.

NAME _____

BONUS AGREEMENT!

SUPER SKILL POWERS • GRADE 3
137

NAME _____

BONUS AGREEMENT!

SUPER SKILL POWERS • GRADE 3
138

MIRACULOUS ADJECTIVES AND ADVERBS!

An **adjective** is a word that describes a noun. Circle the adjective that describes each underlined noun.

Some prairie dogs live in large <u>communities</u> under the ground.

A mother prairie dog makes a nest of dried <u>plants</u> in the spring.

She gives birth to a litter of four <u>pups</u>.

She is a good <u>mother</u> and takes care of her pups.

The pups are ready to venture outside after six <u>weeks</u>.

The pups have many <u>friends</u>.

Write the best adjective from the word bank to complete each sentence.

| rainy | equal | low | tiny |

I put an _____ amount of soup in my bowl and yours.

There is a _____ bug on the leaf.

Latoya stepped over the _____ wall.

She saw a rainbow in the sky on the _____ day.

NAME _____

MIRACULOUS ADJECTIVES AND ADVERBS!

Circle the nouns that the underlined adjectives describe.

My <u>little</u> sister found my stuffed sheep under her pillow.

A <u>new</u> family moved in next door yesterday.

The bear has <u>thick</u>, <u>brown</u> fur.

The <u>chirping</u> birds woke me up this morning.

Her <u>giant</u>, <u>green</u> balloon floated away.

Write an adjective to complete each sentence.

Gabriel showed me the _____ picture.

The _____ puppy is chasing his tail.

That _____ bird flies south for the winter.

Stephen carried the _____ suitcase.

That book with the _____ cover is mine.

SUPER SKILL POWERS • GRADE 3   141

NAME _____

MIRACULOUS ADJECTIVES AND ADVERBS!

Adverbs often modify verbs. Circle the adverb in each sentence. Then, underline the verb that the adverb modifies.

On Independence Day, we usually go to the parade.

We drive slowly because of traffic.

The parade often begins with a marching band.

The marching band plays energetically.

The huge crowd cheers excitedly.

My favorite part is when the big floats pass nearby.

All of the floats are decorated beautifully.

We never see one we don't like.

Write two sentences that use adverbs to describe verbs.

_____

_____

_____

_____

NAME _____

MIRACULOUS ADJECTIVES AND ADVERBS!

Circle the adverb in each sentence. Then, underline the verb each adverb modifies.

The dogs barked loudly at the sound of the doorbell.

I looked everywhere for my coat.

Nancy swims faster than I do.

Greg walked carefully across the old wooden bridge.

Valerie awoke early on Saturday morning.

Let's play outside in the front yard.

Circle the adverb that modifies the underlined verb in each sentence. Then, circle the question the adverb answers about the verb.

The stone skidded playfully across the pond.   How?   When?   Where?

Dad says it's time to come inside.   How?   When?   Where?

Dancers twirled gracefully to the flowing music.   How?   When?   Where?

I saw my favorite teacher today.   How?   When?   Where?

MIRACULOUS ADJECTIVES AND ADVERBS!

Look at each underlined word. On the line, write whether it is a **noun**, **verb**, **adjective**, or **adverb**.

_____ The old green <u>tent</u> smelled of leaves and woodsy air.

_____ Dad <u>quickly</u> unzipped the tent's windows.

_____ The smell of <u>crispy</u> bacon filled the air.

_____ A cool stream <u>ran</u> along one side of the campsite.

_____ <u>Rafael</u> couldn't wait to start the campfire.

_____ We <u>roasted</u> six ears of corn.

List each word on the line beside the correct part of speech.

Seven girls came early.

- noun _____
- verb _____
- adjective _____
- adverb _____

Tall books belong here.

- noun _____
- verb _____
- adjective _____
- adverb _____

The exhausted puppies slept soundly.

- noun _____
- verb _____
- adjective _____
- adverb _____

MIRACULOUS ADJECTIVES AND ADVERBS!

Write the correct forms of each adjective. The first one is done for you.

	Adjectives That Compare Two Nouns	Adjectives That Compare More Than Two Nouns
long	longer	longest
soft		
large		
flat		
sweet		
wide		
cool		

Read the sentences. Circle the correct adjective in parentheses.

4th Annual Fitness Challenge a Success!

Here are the results from last week's Fitness Challenge.

- Brad Dexter and Ariela Vega were the (faster, **fastest**) sprinters.

- The (**youngest**, young) student to participate was six-year-old Emily Yu.

- Most students said the obstacle course this year was (hardest, **harder**) than the one last year.

- Everyone agreed that the (easyest, **easiest**) event was the beanbag toss.

- The weather was both (sunnyer, **sunnier**) and (coldest, **colder**) than last year.

- Morgan Bonaventure won the award for (**Greatest**, Greater) Overall Performance.

NAME _____

MIRACULOUS ADJECTIVES AND ADVERBS!

Complete each sentence with the correct comparative form of the adjective in the box.

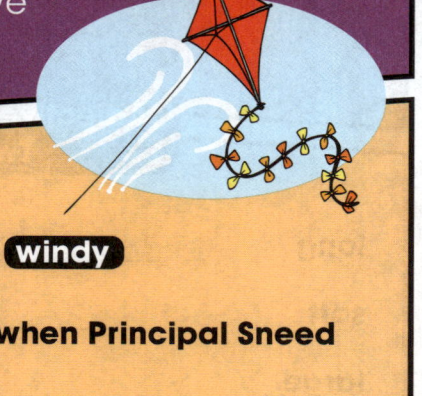

I wish it had been _____ during the Kite Race. **windy**

The _____ cheers came at the end of the day when Principal Sneed did jumping jacks while wearing a suit. **loud**

Micah is _____ than Jack, but Jack can sink more basketballs. **tall**

The _____ race was between Nadia and Kyle. **close**

It is much _____ to ride a bike wearing a helmet than to ride a bike without one. **safe**

This year's awards were even _____ than they have been in other years. **nice**

Follow the directions.

Write a sentence using a comparative adjective to compare two types of animals.

_____

_____

Write a sentence using a comparative adjective to compare two things that you can see from where you are sitting.

_____

_____

NAME _____

MIRACULOUS ADJECTIVES AND ADVERBS!

Fill in the spaces in the chart with the correct adverbs. Remember that some comparative adverbs need to be used with the words **more** or **most**.

	farther	farthest
slowly	_____	more slowly
fast	faster	_____
skillfully	_____	_____
happily	more happily	_____
_____	more patiently	most patiently
_____	_____	latest
safely	_____	most safely
playfully	_____	_____
_____	softer	_____

fast — faster — fastest

NAME _____

MIRACULOUS ADJECTIVES AND ADVERBS!

Read the diary entry. There are seven comparative adverb mistakes. Cross out each mistake. To add a word, use this symbol (^) and write the correct word above it.

Saturday, September 24

Dear Diary,

Today was the first day of Flannery's obedience class. We got there the sooner of all the dogs and owners. Flannery sniffed and greeted the dogs as they arrived. She wagged her tail more cheerfully of all the dogs.

The class leader helped everyone teach their dogs some basic commands. He laughed more harder than even I did when Flannery stole a treat out of his pocket. I'm sure he will hide them carefullier next time. The little dachshund standing next to us fetched the more eagerly of all the dogs. She had short little legs, but she could run more fast than the biggest dog. At the end of the class, Mom and I clapped more loudly of all the owners! Flannery will get her diploma in no time!

MIRACULOUS ADJECTIVES AND ADVERBS!

Read the sentences. The adjective or adverb in each sentence is in purple. On the line below the sentence, write your own sentence. Use a comparative form of the same adjective or adverb. The first one is done for you.

Max lifted the heavy boxes and put them in the moving truck.

An elephant is heavier than a horse.

Nina placed three soft pillows on the bed.

_____

The turtle walked slowly to the pond.

_____

Rory happily waved to his parents.

_____

Will you show me how to make this tasty chili?

_____

My family ate delicious fruit in Hawaii.

_____

The monkeys swung wildly from branch to branch.

_____

NAME _____

ASSESSMENT: ADJECTIVES AND ADVERBS

Circle the nouns that the underlined adjectives describe. **4 pts**

A <u>fluffy</u> bunny sat at the edge of the garden.

The flowers were <u>tall</u> and <u>bright</u> under the sun.

Ants carried <u>heavy</u> loads back to their colonies.

<u>Several</u> bees buzzed around the flower heads.

Circle the adverb that modifies the underlined verb in each sentence. **4 pts**

Yesterday, we <u>walked</u> to the library.

Books were <u>stacked</u> neatly on the racks.

I happily <u>chose</u> two chapter books and checked them out.

I unzipped my backpack and <u>put</u> my books inside.

List each word on the line beside the correct part of speech. **3 pts**

Green trees slowly swayed.

noun _____ adjective _____

verb _____ adverb _____

Ten children ran outside.

noun _____ adjective _____

verb _____ adverb _____

Happy birds sang sweetly.

noun _____ adjective _____

verb _____ adverb _____

SUPER SKILL POWERS • GRADE 3

ASSESSMENT: ADJECTIVES AND ADVERBS

Write the missing comparative adjectives. **6 pts**

fast	_____	_____
_____	_____	tallest
_____	colder	_____
bright	_____	brightest
_____	deeper	_____
kind	_____	_____

Underline an adverb to complete each sentence. **6 pts**

Our puppy plays (more joyfully, joyfuller) with children than anyone else.

Joseph arrived (latest, most late) at the theater.

Please try to whisper (softer, more softly) while the baby sleeps.

Eli jumped (most farthest, farthest) of anyone in the competition.

The stars seem to shine (brightliest, most brightly) far from the city.

My sister completed the craft (carefullier, more carefully) than I did.

YOUR SCORE ___ / 23

19–23 CORRECT ANSWERS = 1 STICKER

NAME _____

BONUS ADJECTIVES AND ADVERBS!

As you read on your own, pay attention to adjectives and adverbs. In each comic strip frame, write a different adjective or adverb from your reading. Then, write the comparative and superlative forms of each.

| beautiful | more beautiful | most beautiful |

NAME _____

BONUS ADJECTIVES AND ADVERBS!

SUPER SKILL POWERS • GRADE 3

153

NAME _____

BONUS ADJECTIVES AND ADVERBS!

SPELLBINDING SENTENCES!

A **clause** is a group of words that has a subject and a verb. Sometimes, a clause is a complete thought and can be a sentence all by itself. Sometimes, a clause is an incomplete thought and needs another clause to make a sentence. Read the clauses below. If the clause is a complete thought, make a check mark (✔) on the line. If it is an incomplete thought, make an ✘ on the line. The first two are done for you.

✔ The movie was fantastic

✘ If we go to the zoo

_____ Our dog Ralph chases his own tail

_____ Because it was too early in the morning

_____ When the ball flew into the neighbors' yard

_____ Delaney jumped over the puddle

_____ Although we had fun at the park

_____ If you are not careful

_____ The baseball game lasted four hours

_____ Because Jamie left the door open

SPELLBINDING SENTENCES!

A **simple sentence** has one subject and one verb. It is a clause that expresses a complete thought. Read each simple sentence below. Underline the simple subject (the noun or pronoun only), and circle the verb. The first one is done for you.

<u>Mr. Bennett</u> (reads) the newspaper.

James had a sore throat yesterday.

The race started right on time.

Oranges are my favorite fruit.

I washed the car after breakfast.

Lily asked for corn on the cob.

Write two simple sentences of your own. Each should have only one clause.

_____
_____
_____
_____

NAME _____

SPELLBINDING SENTENCES!

A **compound sentence** is two simple sentences (or clauses) joined together with a coordinating conjunction like **and**, **but**, **or**, or **so**. Read each compound sentence below. Circle the coordinating conjunction that joins the two clauses.

The kids rode their bikes to the ice cream shop, but it was closed.

Two squirrels raced around the tree, and a cat watched them closely.

It was raining pretty hard, so recess was held indoors.

We could go to the school play, or we could go to the volleyball game.

Combine each pair of simple sentences to write compound sentences. Use the conjunction shown in parentheses. Do not forget to write a comma before the conjunction in each sentence.

We might go to the park. We might go to the store. (or)
_____
_____

My dog is ready to play. My cat wants to nap. (but)
_____
_____

It may rain tonight. The party will be indoors. (so)
_____
_____

158 SUPER SKILL POWERS • GRADE 3

NAME _____

SPELLBINDING SENTENCES!

Add a simple sentence after each conjunction below to form a compound sentence. The first one is done for you.

Mr. Sanchez is a teacher, but
Mr. Sanchez is a teacher, but he doesn't work at my school.

Dad is teaching Omar how to mow the lawn, but
_____

Hannah feeds the cats each morning, or
_____

It is supposed to snow on Tuesday, so
_____

Beatrix just joined the swim team, and
_____

Write three compound sentences of your own. For each sentence, use one of the conjunctions from the box. Remember to add a comma before each conjunction.

| and | but | or | so |

_____
_____
_____
_____
_____

NAME _____

SPELLBINDING SENTENCES!

Read each sentence. On the line, write **S** if it is a simple sentence or **C** if it is a compound sentence.

_____ Tomorrow, our soccer team plays the first game of the season.

_____ Mario bought a model airplane, and Lita bought a box of markers.

_____ Spaghetti is Aunt Maggie's favorite food of all.

_____ Grandma is taking my sister and me to the beach.

_____ The tent was left unzipped, so mosquitoes got in.

_____ Dad jogged, and Linden rode his bike beside him.

_____ Lisa helped make the costumes for the musical.

_____ Everyone wanted pie, but there was only one slice left.

_____ This morning, I woke up before dawn.

_____ After dinner, my whole family went for a walk.

NAME _____

SPELLBINDING SENTENCES!

A **complex sentence** is two simple sentences joined together with a subordinating conjunction like **because**, **if**, **when**, or **although**. Read each complex sentence below. Circle the subordinating conjunction that makes the two clauses into one sentence.

Rafiq could not see the whiteboard although he sat in the front row.

We lit candles last night because the electricity went out.

Eliza's bike got a flat tire when she rode over a nail.

I can spend the night at your house if I finish cleaning my room.

Add a subordinating conjunction to the beginning or middle of each incomplete sentence to make a complex sentence.

_____ the lines were so long, the students did not see the mummy exhibit.

_____ you hold your bag on your lap, you will not lose it.

Shel could not get his homework finished _____ someone was hammering.

_____ everyone was very quiet, nobody heard Mr. Wong's footsteps in the hallway.

The race will begin _____ all the runners are in place at the starting line.

_____ the big hand is on the 12, it will be 10 o'clock.

NAME _____

SPELLBINDING SENTENCES!

Add a simple sentence after each conjunction below to form a compound sentence. The first one is done for you.

When _we started third grade_ we had no idea it would be so much fun.

If _____,
the cat will stop meowing.

The train began to move although
_____.

Everyone scurried inside because
_____.

Write three complex sentences of your own. For each sentence, use one of the conjunctions from the box. Remember that a clause starting with a subordinating conjunction can be the first or second part of a complex sentence.

_____
_____
_____
_____
_____
_____

SPELLBINDING SENTENCES!

Read each sentence. On the line, write **C** if it is a compound sentence or **CX** if it is a complex sentence.

_____ The sun was really bright at the zoo, so I wore my sunglasses all day.

_____ Bats like dark places, so they often live in caves.

_____ Because monkeys like to swing, their habitat includes tree branches and metal bars.

_____ The caretaker fed the seals raw fish, and we got to watch.

_____ Giraffes make funny noises when they chew.

_____ If a male peacock has very beautiful feathers, the female will like him better.

_____ Although many fish can swim together in the aquarium, some have to be kept separate.

_____ We could keep watching the fish, or we could visit the alligators and crocodiles.

_____ The baby zebras were cute, but the penguins were my favorite.

_____ I like the penguins best because they seem to be wearing tuxedos.

SPELLBINDING SENTENCES!

Read each sentence below. On the line, write **C** if it is a compound sentence or **CX** if it is a complex sentence.

_____ The hummingbird drank from a flower, and then it flew away.

_____ When Billy got to the park on Saturday, Rajul was waiting for him.

_____ Because Lucia has a beautiful voice, she's going to take singing lessons this fall.

_____ Sarah plays basketball every day, so she will probably beat you in a game of Horse.

_____ The plants were okay although the temperature dropped last night.

_____ Ansel stopped at the library, but the book he ordered wasn't in yet.

SPELLBINDING SENTENCES!

Read each sentence. On the line, write **S** if it is a simple sentence, **C** if it is a compound sentence, and **CX** if it is a complex sentence. Then, underline each conjunction in the compound and complex sentences.

_____ When school starts, Jada wants a new backpack.

_____ The car wouldn't start because the battery was too cold.

_____ Mr. O'Rourke retired from teaching last year.

_____ If you finish your homework, we will be able to watch the movie.

_____ Owen and Rosie are going camping today, but they'll be back on Sunday.

_____ Anton will lose his place in line if he goes to buy a snack.

_____ We can cook chicken, or we can go out for dinner.

_____ Although I like to ride my bike, I'm going to roller-skate to Jenna's house today.

_____ Nazim is going to vacuum, and Molly is going to dust.

_____ Because Gabriela lost the book, she'll have to pay a fine.

ASSESSMENT: SENTENCES

If the conjunction is a coordinating conjunction for making compound sentences, write **C** on the line. If it is a subordinating conjunction for making complex sentences, write **CX** on the line.

8 pts

_____ although   _____ if

_____ and   _____ or

_____ because   _____ so

_____ but   _____ when

Read the compound and complex sentences below. Underline the two simple sentences that make up each one. Then, circle the coordinating or subordinating conjunction.

6 pts

When we get off the bus, we will go straight to the museum.

If there is enough to go around, everyone can try the homemade bread.

Cars sped down the highway, but the nearby train was stuck on the tracks.

Students can participate in the spelling bee, or they can sign up for the math challenge.

No one was allowed to wade through the creek because the water was so deep.

Helen is our team's goalie, and Irena is the other team's goalie.

ASSESSMENT: SENTENCES

Read each sentence. On the line, write **S** if it is a simple sentence, **C** if it is a compound sentence, and **CX** if it is a complex sentence.

10 pts

_____ Carrots are Charlotte's favorite food.

_____ Kent swam across the pool to the ladder.

_____ Singing in the chorus is fun, but I would rather have a solo.

_____ Mr. Keane's job was to keep everyone in the auditorium quiet.

_____ Samantha loves blowing bubbles, so I got her a giant bubble wand for her birthday.

_____ My grandmother's name is Mary, and my grandfather's name is James.

_____ The car keys are hanging on the hook by the door, or they are in Mom's purse.

_____ When I get up tomorrow morning, I have to rake the leaves.

_____ If your shoes are too small, you will get blisters.

_____ The driveway was flooded because it poured rain all night.

_____ Although Dad practiced all afternoon, he still could not make a three-point shot.

YOUR SCORE ___/24

19–24 CORRECT ANSWERS = 1 STICKER

NAME _____

BONUS SENTENCES!

Practice making complex sentences. Whenever you do an activity, write a simple sentence that describes it. Then, add a clause that begins with **although**, **because**, **if**, or **when** to provide more detail. Finally, draw a vertical line between the two clauses.

Stella and I jumped rope | although we really wanted to go swimming.

NAME _____

BONUS SENTENCES!

NAME _____

CAPTIVATING VOCABULARY!

When a prefix is added to a base word, it changes the meaning of the word. Circle the prefix in each word. Then, write the letter of the correct definition next to the word.

_____ reopen

_____ unhappy

_____ misplace

_____ unsure

_____ misuse

A. to wrongly place

B. not happy

C. to wrongly use

D. to open again

E. not sure

Add the prefix **un-** or **re-** to each word. Then, write the meaning of each new word.

sure _____

happy _____

able _____

write _____

tell _____

print _____

NAME _____

CAPTIVATING VOCABULARY!

Circle the root word in each word below. Then, think of another word that has the same root. Write the new word on the line.

unreasonable _____

disinterested _____

misbehaving _____

unbelievable _____

bicycling _____

telephone _____

disagreeable _____

misspelled _____

distrustful _____

microscope _____

NAME _____

CAPTIVATING VOCABULARY!

Underline the suffix in each word. Then, write the word's definition on the line.

hopeful _____

careless _____

happiest _____

wonderful _____

likable _____

greatest _____

beautiful _____

helpless _____

Now, write three of your own sentences. Use one word from above in each sentence.

_____
_____
_____
_____
_____
_____

NAME _____

CAPTIVATING VOCABULARY!

Read each pair of words. For each pair, write one way the two things are alike and one way they are different.

leopard, cheetah _____
_____

keyboard, piano _____
_____

cabin, tent _____
_____

whistle, sing _____
_____

Circle the word that does not belong in each group of words. Then, describe why the other words belong together.

tuba, clarinet, jazz, flute, harp _____

tire, hammer, screwdriver, wrench _____

robin, hawk, sparrow, dog, crow _____

Moon, Mars, Earth, Jupiter, Venus _____

lettuce, peach, carrot, peas, beets _____

rose, daisy, lazy, tulip, lily _____

CAPTIVATING VOCABULARY!

Read each group of related words. Write two more related words for each group. The first one is done for you.

robin, owl, pigeon   quail   pheasant

peaches, apples, pears

spoon, bowl, cup

lake, pond, river

branches, sticks, wood

lemonade, water, milk

dollar, dime, penny

carrot, celery, cucumber

dress, shoes, skirt

tennis, golf, racquetball

CAPTIVATING VOCABULARY!

Read each pair of words. If they are synonyms, write **S** on the line. If they are antonyms, write **A**.

_____ ancient modern   _____ imitate copy

_____ assist help   _____ combine separate

_____ increase decrease   _____ lucky fortunate

_____ enlarge magnify   _____ frequent seldom

_____ accept refuse   _____ patient impatient

_____ bitter sweet   _____ genuine real

Write the correct word from the word bank on each line to complete the passage.

| plant | heat | sunlight | Earth | oxygen | plants |

Sunlight is very important to our planet, _____ .

Most of our food comes from _____ life.

_____ also give off the _____ we breathe. Without _____, plants would die, and we would not have food or air.

The _____ of the sun also warms Earth. Without it, we would freeze.

NAME _____

CAPTIVATING VOCABULARY!

Read the story. Then, write the meaning of each word.

Gabe lives in a large city with his grandparents. The building his family lives in is tall and has different sets of rooms for each family that lives there. This building is called an apartment building. In this urban area, the buildings are close together. People do not have to go far to get things they need. Gabe's cousin Jasper lives in a rural, or country, community. He plays in his backyard instead of in a park like Gabe. There is a lot of space between houses where Jasper lives. Jasper's parents must drive serveral miles to go shopping.

community _____

urban _____

rural _____

Use context clues to figure out the meaning of each underlined word. Circle the letter of the correct definition.

Anna was <u>eager</u> for the basketball game to start. She was ready to show off her new skills.
a. afraid
b. excited
c. sad

Clark wanted to go out for pizza, but he was <u>flexible</u>. Anyplace with good food was fine with him.
a. able to lift heavy objects
b. able to try new things
c. able to be bent

CAPTIVATING VOCABULARY!

Complete each sentence using one of the words below. Each word will be used only once.

bank   play   ball   kid   park   fly   run   bat

The kitten watched the _____ crawl slowly up the wall.

You wouldn't _____ me, would you? asked Dad.

Do you think Aunt Donna and Uncle Mike will come to my school _____?

He hit the ball so hard it broke the _____.

"My favorite part of the story is when the princess goes to the _____," sighed Veronica.

My brother scored the first _____ in the game.

Before we go to the store, I want to get some coins out of my _____.

Is it okay to _____ my bike here?

SUPER SKILL POWERS • GRADE 3

NAME _____

CAPTIVATING VOCABULARY!

Now, use each each word from the previous page in a new way in the sentences below.

bank   play   ball   kid   park   fly   run   bat

We will have to _____ quietly while the baby is sleeping.

The nature center will bring a live _____ for our class to see.

We sat on the _____ as we fished in the river.

The umpire decided the pitcher needed a new _____.

We will _____ in a race tomorrow.

"Can we please go to the _____ after I clean my room?" asked Jordan.

That boomerang can really _____!

The baby goat, or _____, follows its mother everywhere.

CAPTIVATING VOCABULARY!

Some words can be a noun at one time and a verb at another time. Complete each pair of sentences below with a word from the box. The word will be a noun in the first sentence and a verb in the second sentence.

| mix | kiss | brush | crash |

Did your dog ever give you a _____ ?

I have a cold, so I can't _____ you today.

I brought my comb and my _____ .

I will _____ the leaves off your coat.

Was anyone hurt in the _____ ?

If you aren't careful, you will _____ into me.

We bought a cake _____ at the store.

I will _____ the eggs together.

NAME _____

ASSESSMENT: VOCABULARY

Write the meaning of each word on the line. **8 pts**

unable _____

rewrite _____

misuse _____

displeased _____

hopeful _____

likable _____

careless _____

unlikable _____

Underline the root in each word. **8 pts**

uninteresting   painless

telescope   wonderful

reasonable   unhappily

tricycle   rereading

NAME _____

ASSESSMENT: VOCABULARY

Circle the word that does not belong in each group. **4 pts**

grapes, beans, apples, cherries, oranges

football, soccer, volleyball, tennis, freeze tag

ocean, river, mountain, stream, creek

Orlando, Saturn, Mercury, Neptune, Uranus

Write **S** next to each pair of synonyms. Write **A** next to each pair of antonyms. **6 pts**

_____ sweet sour	_____ accept refuse
_____ lucky unlucky	_____ inform misinform
_____ seldom rarely	_____ help aid

Complete each sentence with a word from the word bank. Some words will be used more than once. **6 pts**

bat   park   run   fly

Let's go to the _____ and ride the merry-go-round!

The batter who was on second base scored a _____.

Your mom can _____ in our driveway.

The _____ buzzing around my ear is driving me crazy!

Did you _____ or drive to Toronto?

For Halloween, I dressed up as a vampire _____.

YOUR SCORE ___/32

26–32 CORRECT ANSWERS = 1 STICKER

BONUS VOCABULARY!

Think of words you know that have multiple meanings. Write one of these words in each comic strip frame. Then, draw two pictures two show two different meanings of the word.

NAME

BONUS VOCABULARY!

SUPER SKILL POWERS • GRADE 3

NAME _____

BONUS VOCABULARY!

POWERFUL PUNCTUATION!

Read the paragraphs. Put an **X** over the six incorrect periods or question marks. Add the correct end marks, and circle them. The first one is done for you.

Have you ever visited the Sleeping Bear Dunes(?) They are located along the shore of Lake Michigan. The enormous dunes, or sand hills, are more than 400 feet tall in places. Many people travel to Michigan every year to climb the dunes? Most visitors come in the summer, but some people come in the winter instead. Why would they visit the icy shores of the lake in the winter. Sledding down the steep slopes can be a lot of fun!

Do you know where the dunes got their name. A Native American legend says that a mother bear lay on the beach to watch for her cubs after a fire. Over time, sand covered the bear? Some people still think they can see the shape of a bear sleeping on the beach. This is how the dunes came to be called the Sleeping Bear Dunes?

POWERFUL PUNCTUATION!

An exclamatory sentence shows strong emotions or feelings. Write **E** for each exclamatory sentence. Write **D** for each declarative sentence. Write **I** for each interrogative sentence.

_____ What did they say?   _____ I am so happy for you!

_____ It's a boy!   _____ That is wonderful news!

_____ The card is green.   _____ Can I borrow a pencil?

Write three sentences. Use a word from the word bank in each sentence. Use capital letters, periods, question marks, and exclamation points where they are needed.

| adult | during | finish | interested | job | prepare | summer | work |

_____

_____

_____

_____

_____

_____

POWERFUL PUNCTUATION!

Add the correct end mark to each sentence. You should add four periods, two question marks, and three exclamation points.

Evan and Tanner have been jumping on the trampoline all morning___

Have you read the book <u>A Cricket in Times Square</u>___

Kazuki's swimming lesson was canceled___

Watch out___

Please clean your room before bedtime___

The Broadview Tigers won the championship___

Would you like cheese on your sandwich___

There's a huge spider in my bed___

Tara traded stickers with her little brother___

Write a sentence that shows excitement. Your sentence should end with an exclamation point.

_____
_____

NAME _____

POWERFUL PUNCTUATION!

There are two choices below for each item. Choose the correct version, and write the letter in the space.

_____ a. Omaha, NE
b. Omaha NE

_____ a. Amarillo Texas
b. Amarillo, Texas

_____ a. Nashville, Tennessee, is 284 miles from Shreveport, Louisiana.
b. Nashville Tennessee, is 284 miles from Shreveport, Louisiana.

_____ a. Our class took a field trip to, Boston, Massachusetts, last year.
b. Our class took a field trip to Boston, Massachusetts, last year.

Ask two people in your class or your family the questions below. Record their answers on the lines. Use commas correctly.

In what city and state were you born?

_____

_____

What city and country would you most like to visit?

_____

_____

SUPER SKILL POWERS • GRADE 3   191

POWERFUL PUNCTUATION!

Add the missing commas to each address below. Use this symbol to add them: ⁀.

19052 Tanglewood Dr.

Rocky River, OH 44116

133 Greenvale Rd.

Lincoln, NE 68516

958 East Oak Lane #17

Baltimore, MD 21218

21896 Sardis Court

Portland, OR 97215

35 Frog Creek Woods

Harrisburg, PA 17111

568 Elm Street

Colton, CA 92324

NAME _____

POWERFUL PUNCTUATION!

For each address below, make a check mark (✓) on the line if it uses commas correctly. Make an ✗ if it uses commas incorrectly.

_____ Ms. Reba Masters
223 Hornbeam Ln.
Silver Springs, NY, 14550

_____ Miss Penelope Price
661 Midas Touch, Ct.
Waverly TN 37185

_____ Mr. Carlton Jones
7251 Roaming Rooster Rd.
Greensburg, PA 15601

_____ Mr. Ronald Speck
22 Tangerine Ln.
Barberville FL, 32105

_____ Dr. Alexis Curran
321 E. Moody St.
Dearborn, MI 48121

_____ Mr. Ellis Case
101 N. Grove St.
Dexter, ME 04930

Write your full address. Then, write a friend's full address. Use commas correctly.

Name _____
Street address _____
City/State/Zip code _____
Name _____
Street address _____
City/State/Zip code _____

SUPER SKILL POWERS • GRADE 3

POWERFUL PUNCTUATION!

To add commas where they are needed in the dialogue below, use a mark like this: ⁀.

"I'd like to ride the Ferris wheel first" said Anya.

"I'll meet you over there" said Kahlil "after I get something to drink."

"The fair seems even more crowded this year than last" commented Riley.

"My favorite attraction is the bumper cars" said Jacob "but I also love the giant slides."

"I can't go on anything that spins" said Kahlil "because it makes me feel sick."

Riley pointed and said "There's the frozen lemonade stand."

Anya asked "What time are you meeting your parents?"

"The line is too long for the rocket ship ride" decided Oliver.

POWERFUL PUNCTUATION!

Quotation marks set off what someone says. Write quotation marks in each sentence around what each person says. Use this symbol to add quotation marks: ". The first one is done for you.

Uncle Neil said, "I will pack a picnic lunch."

Where is the big beach ball? asked Jeff.

Ilene exclaimed, That is a wonderful idea!

Come and do your work, Grandma said, or you can't go with us.

Yesterday, said Ella, I saw a pretty robin in the tree by my window.

I will always take care of my pets, promised Theodore.

Rachel said, Maybe we should have practiced more.

Dr. Jacobs asked, How are you, Pat?

POWERFUL PUNCTUATION!

Read each sentence below. If the sentence is correct, make a check mark on the line (✓). If it is not correct, make an ✗ on the line. Then, use the proofreading marks in the box to show the changes. The first one is done for you.

⌃,	= insert comma
⊙	= insert period
⌃"	= insert quotation marks

___✗___ "Our suitcases are in the attic⌃," said Dad⊙

_____ This summer, I am going to take Spanish lessons, said Mackenzie.

_____ "My family is driving all the way across the country in an RV," Ryan said.

_____ Nicolae said "I plan to go swimming at the lake every day

Add commas, quotation marks, and periods where they are needed. Use the proofreading marks above.

"Did you know that Reid lives in Dallas, Texas?

"Mr. Jarvis is my neighbor said Grandma

Is Caden's birthday in April?" asked Sasha.

"My mother and I shop at Smith's Market" I added.

What is your favorite month of the year? asked Rosie

POWERFUL PUNCTUATION!

The sentences below are missing commas, periods, and quotation marks. Rewrite each sentence. Add punctuation marks where needed.

I have never been to a farm before replied Audrey

Neither have I agreed Norah

My grandparents have cows, horses, goats, and barn cats said Van

He added I stay with them every summer, and there is always something to do

I would love to learn how to ride a horse or milk a cow said Audrey

Van grinned at Audrey and said My grandparents can always use an extra hand

ASSESSMENT: PUNCTUATION

Add a period, question mark, or exclamation point to each sentence.

8 pts

I cannot believe how absolutely amazing the weather is today ___

Do you have any brothers or sisters ___

Every year, our school plants a tree ___

I am going to a birthday party next weekend ___

Watch out ___

When will we learn about Mars ___

I heard about the changes to the lunch menu ___

Is the juice on the counter for me ___

Add commas, quotation marks, and periods where they are needed. Use the proofreading marks in the box.

4 pts

"Let's go to the movies later, said Marcus.

Andrew said "That table looks like it's about to fall"

Is there something wrong with your sandwich? asked Ms. Skinner.

The store is filled with Thanksgiving shoppers," said the reporter

ˆ,	= insert comma
⊙	= insert period
⌄⌄	= insert quotation marks

ASSESSMENT: PUNCTUATION

Add commas where they are needed. Use this proofreading mark: ⁀.

4 pts

The Rock and Roll Hall of Fame is in Cleveland, Ohio.

Sarah Hughes skated in the Winter Olympics in Salt Lake City, Utah.

In 2012, Bradley Wiggins won the Tour de France in Liege, Belgium.

Olympic swimmer Michael Phelps was born in Baltimore, Maryland in 1985.

Add the missing commas to each address. Use this proofreading mark: ⁀.

4 pts

81 Riverwood Rd.
Charlotte, NC 28870

1425 Newtown Terrace
Providence, RI 02906

132 West Billingsley Lane
Taos, NM 87571

21896 Langston Blvd.
San Diego, CA 92119

YOUR SCORE ___ / 20

16–20 CORRECT ANSWERS = 1 STICKER

BONUS PUNCTUATION!

Practice punctuating dialogue. Listen to what friends and family members say. Then, in each comic strip frame, write a sentence you heard. Add commas and quotation marks where needed.

"We don't have time to stop for ice cream," said Mom.

NAME _____

BONUS PUNCTUATION!

BONUS PUNCTUATION!

NAME _____

EXCEPTIONAL SPELLING!

Circle the misspelled word in each set. Then, write the correct spelling on the line.

again	anuther	always	_____
body	bring	bilt	_____
community	continant	country	_____
deside	describe	different	_____
enough	everything	especielly	_____
favorite	feeld	finally	_____
goes	great	groop	_____
heart	hole	hapy	_____
idea	iland	impossible	_____
money	morning	moove	_____

EXCEPTIONAL SPELLING!

Circle the word that correctly completes each sentence.

I Like Art

I like to (learn, lern, lurn) about all kinds of things in (scool, skool, school).

Still, art is my (favorite, faverite, favorit) subject. We (nevver, never, nehver) have to take a quiz or test in art class. Instead, we just (werk, work, worc) on our art projects. We don't (olways, allways, always) draw or paint a (picture, pichure, pictcher). We also make (uhther, uther, other) kinds of artwork. We make shapes with clay, and weave yarn to make cloth. After we have (dun, done, donne) a lot of different kinds of projects, we go back to painting (aggin, again, agen).

EXCEPTIONAL SPELLING!

Circle the word that correctly completes each sentence.

My Favorite Restaurant

My favorite (plase, plais, **place**) to eat lunch is a small restaurant in

the (senter, cinter, **center**) of the city. Ever (**since**, cinse, sense) my older

sister first took me there, I've really liked it. The food is simple but very good.

I usually get a bowl of (ries, **rice**, rise) and vegetables covered with a sweet

(sause, **sauce**, saus) . The cook adds exactly the amount of (spies, spise, **spice**)

I like in my food.

The restaurant has a quiet patio in the back. My sister and I enjoy

the (**silence**, cilense, silents) of the patio and drink (**juice**, juiss, juis)

before we eat. Then, our server writes down our lunch order with a pad

and (pensil, **pencil**, pensle) . When we change our minds, he has to

(**erase**, erais, erase) the order and write it again.

NAME _____

EXCEPTIONAL SPELLING!

Fill in the blanks with **c** or **s** to complete the words with the /s/ sound.

Do you have enough spa____e to do your dan____e routine?

I can't believe you jumped over the fen____e!

We rode our bikes ____uper fa____t.

Cary threw the ball of paper but mi____ ____ed the trash can.

The batter made it to first ba____e.

Did Matt ride the ____ity bu____ to the play?

Circle the correctly spelled word in each set. Then, write it on the line.

chance	chans	chanse	_____
sycle	cycle	sicle	_____
piece	peise	piess	_____
addrese	addres	address	_____
mooss	moose	mooce	_____

SUPER SKILL POWERS • GRADE 3   **207**

NAME _____

EXCEPTIONAL SPELLING!

Add the ending shown to each base word to make a new word. Don't forget to change the spelling of the base word when the ending is added.

change y to i

try + s = _____

happy + ness = _____

double the final consonant

sit + ing = _____

hop + ed = _____

drop the final e

smile + ed = _____

slide + ing = _____

change ie to y or y to ie

lie + ing = _____

puppy + s = _____

Each word below contains the suffix **est**, **tion**, or **ty**. Circle each suffix. Then, write the base word. The first one is done for you.

safe(ty)   _____safe_____   saddest   _____

hungriest _____   action   _____

invention _____   tasty   _____

certainly _____   loyalty   _____

direction _____   suggestion _____

loveliest _____   surest   _____

208 SUPER SKILL POWERS • GRADE 3

EXCEPTIONAL SPELLING!

Write the word that correctly completes each tongue twister.

My mom is (makeing, making, macking) many more muffins.

Henry (hopped, hopeed, hoped) his horse hadn't hurt her hoof.

Six ships sailed south under the (shinying, shining, shinning) summer sun.

Ben (baked, bakied, bakked) bread before beginning to broil the beef.

Skip sledded, skied, and (skated, skatted, skateed) on some slippery surfaces.

Dan discovered a dozen (divving, diveing, diving) dolphins.

Hundreds of hens were (hideing, hiding, hidying) from hungry hunters.

Harry is (having, havving, haveing) his helper hold his hat.

Hefty hikers (hiked, hikeed, hikied) happily up the highest hill.

Rodrick will be (ridding, ridying, riding) the red rubber racehorse.

EXCEPTIONAL SPELLING!

Circle the word in each pair that is correctly divided into syllables. Use the dictionary in the back if you need help.

dinner	di-nner	din-ner
traffic	tra-ffic	traf-fic
possible	pos-si-ble	po-ssib-le
soccer	so-ccer	soc-cer
tomorrow	to-mor-row	tom-orr-ow
buffalo	buff-al-o	buf-fa-lo
collect	co-llect	col-lect
beginning	be-ginn-ing	be-gin-ning
annoy	an-noy	a-nnoy
address	add-ress	ad-dress

EXCEPTIONAL SPELLING!

Circle the word that correctly completes each sentence.

Shopping Trip

Last weekend, I went to the mall to shop. I dropped a (leter, **letter**, ledder) in the mailbox for my mother on my way to the mall. When I got there, I walked around looking in the shop windows. I saw a nice jacket, but I didn't like the (**zipper**, ziper, zipber) on the front. I like buttons (**better**, bedder, beter). I also saw some funny slippers that were each shaped like a (rabit, rabitt, **rabbit**) with long, floppy ears. They were on sale for only a (**dollar**, dolear, dolar), so I bought them. I also bought some (socker, **soccer**, socer) cleats.

When I got to the last shop, I saw a man on a tall (lader, latter, **ladder**) using a (hamer, **hammer**, hamner) to nail a sign over the door. I was afraid that an accident would (**happen**, haphen, hapenn) if I walked under him. So, I decided to go home. It was almost time to eat (dinier, **dinner**, diner) anyway.

NAME _____

ASSESSMENT: SPELLING

Circle the misspelled word in each set. Then, write the correct spelling on the line.

5 pts

boddy	continent	everything	_____
ziper	rabbit	hammer	_____
move	heart	favorit	_____
dollar	hapen	great	_____
another	monie	finally	_____

Fill in the blanks with **c** or **s** to complete the words with the /s/ sound.

5 pts

Please hand me that pen____il.

The silen____e in the library made me sleepy.

Era____e the problem and try again.

Did you make it to home ba____e in time?

I can't wait to show off my new dan____e moves!

Add the ending shown to each base word.

8 pts

fly + s = _____   kitty + s = _____

file + ed = _____   lie + ing = _____

ride + ing = _____   fit + ing = _____

shop + ed = _____   happy + ness = _____

YOUR SCORE ____ / 18

15–18 CORRECT ANSWERS = 1 STICKER

212 SUPER SKILL POWERS • GRADE 3

NAME _____

BONUS SPELLING!

Practice spelling words with double consonants. Anytime you find a word with a double consonant in your own reading, write the word in a comic strip frame. Then, draw a picture to represent the word.

SUPER SKILL POWERS • GRADE 3   213

NAME _____

BONUS SPELLING!

NAME _____

BONUS SPELLING!

SUPER SKILL POWERS • GRADE 3

ANSWER KEY

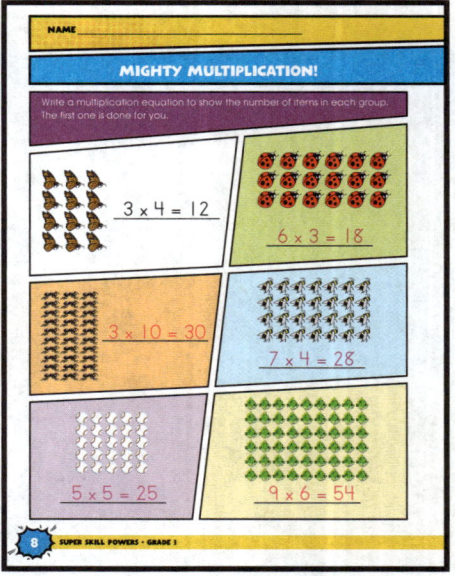
Page 8

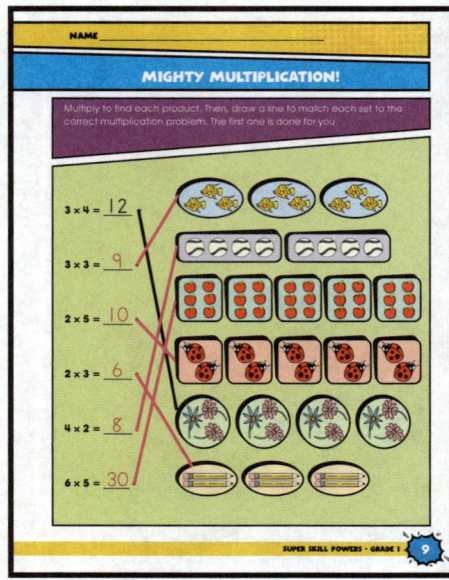
Page 9

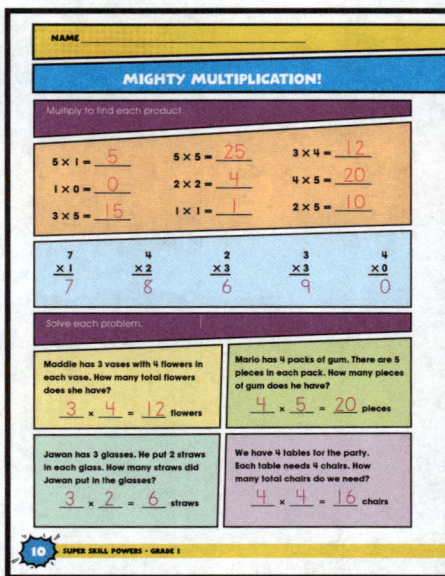
Page 10

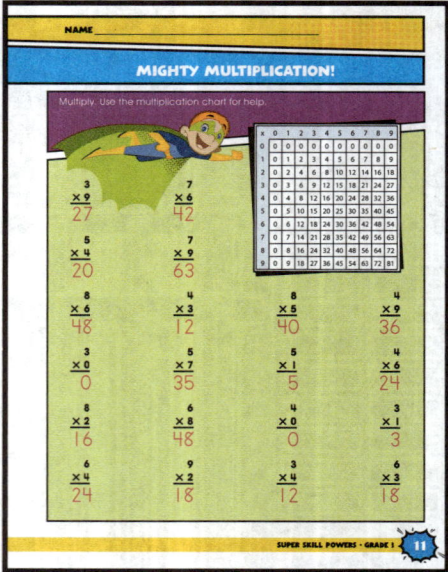
Page 11

Page 12

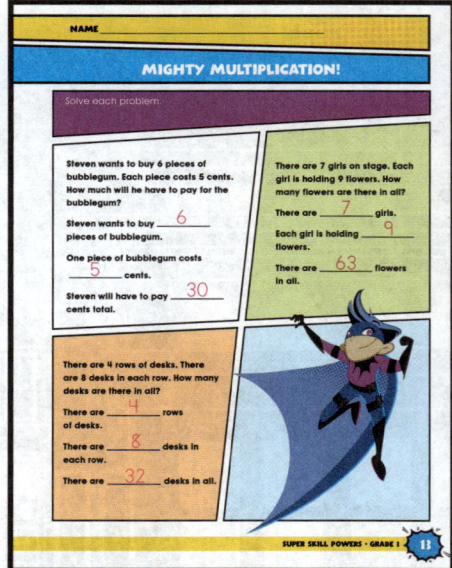
Page 13

ANSWER KEY

Page 14

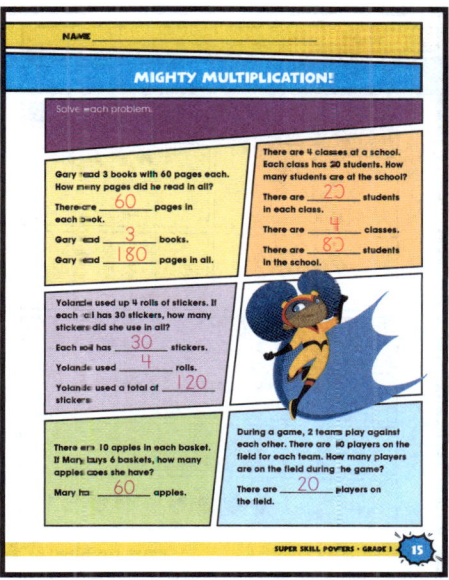

Page 15

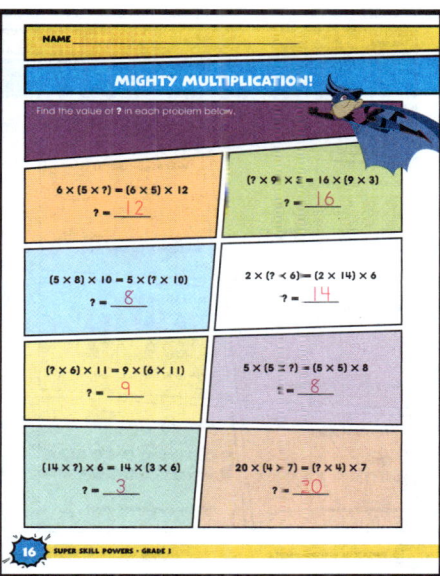

Page 16

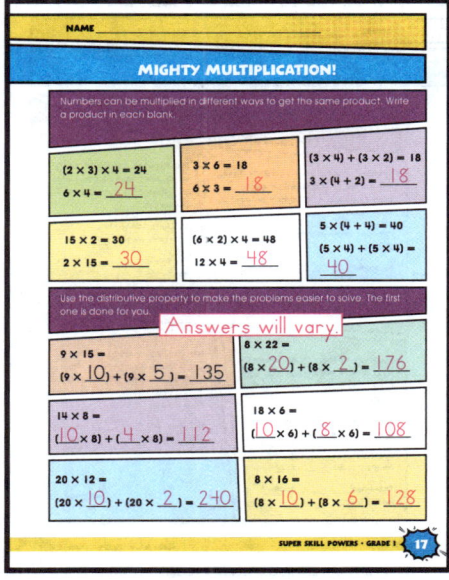

Page 17

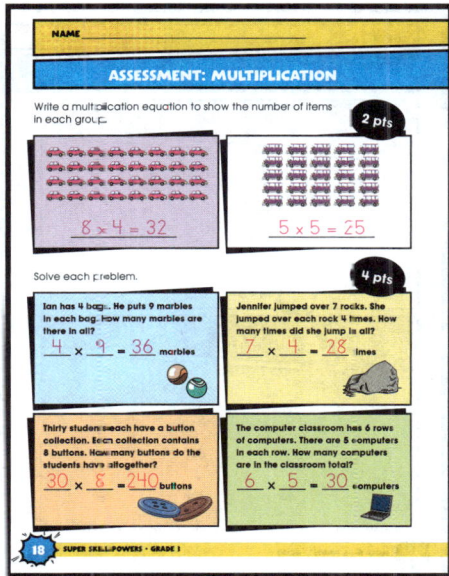

Page 18

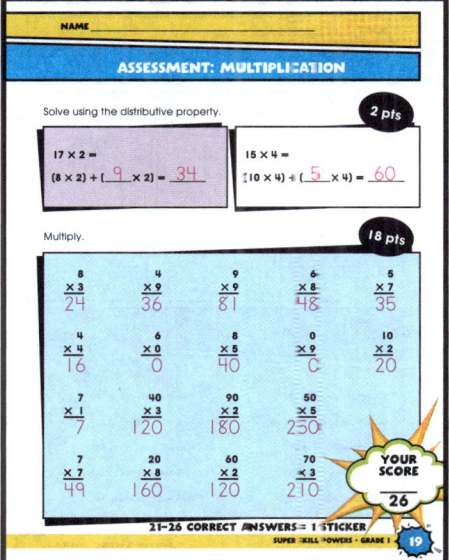

Page 19

ANSWER KEY

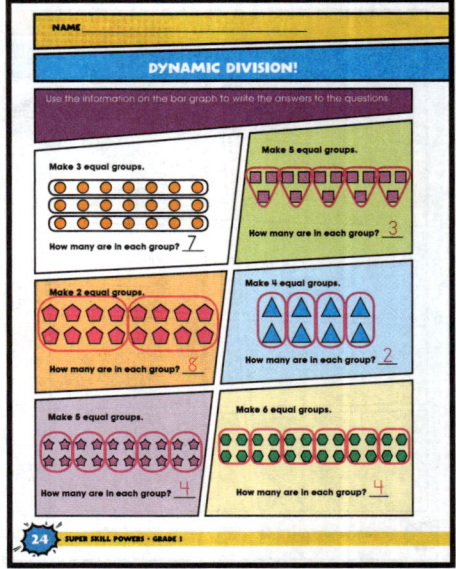
Page 24

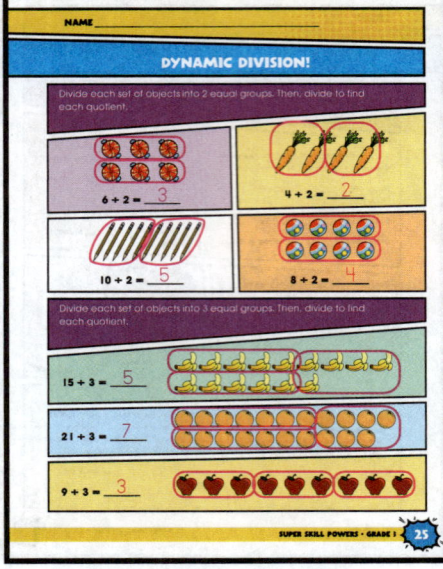
Page 25

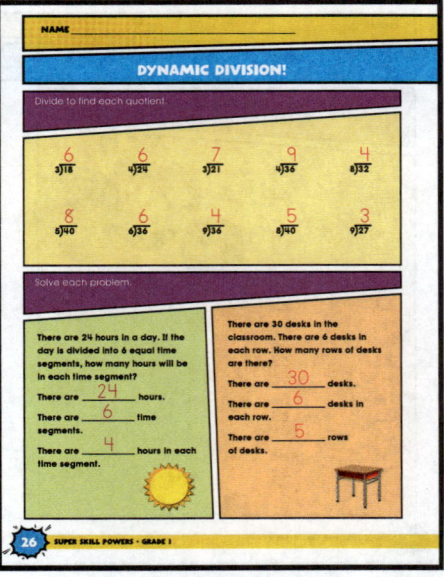
Page 26

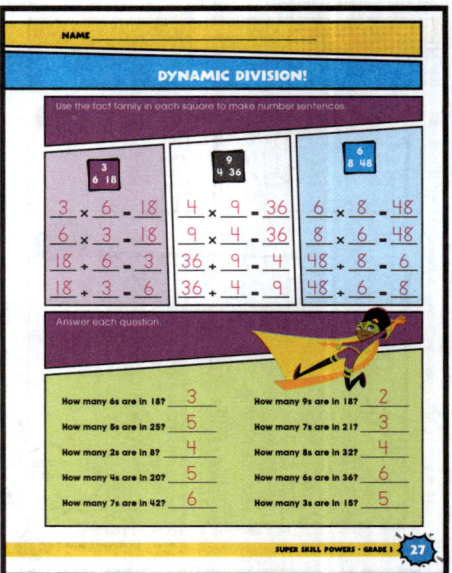
Page 27

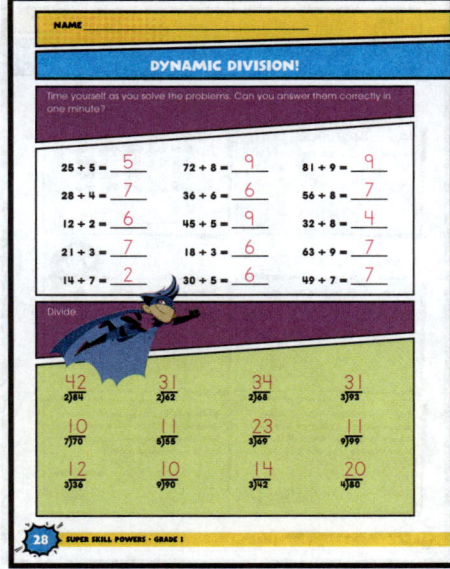
Page 28

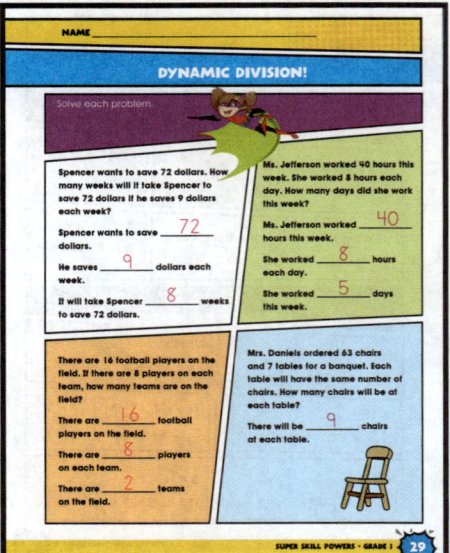
Page 29

ANSWER KEY

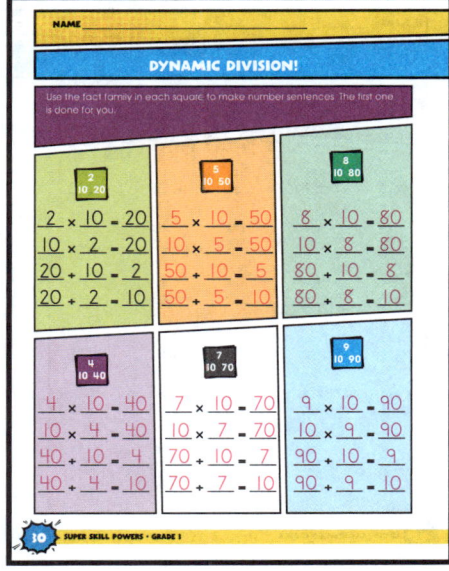
Page 30

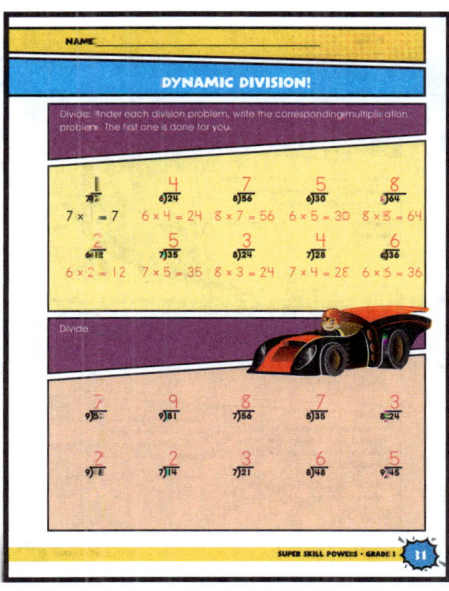
Page 31

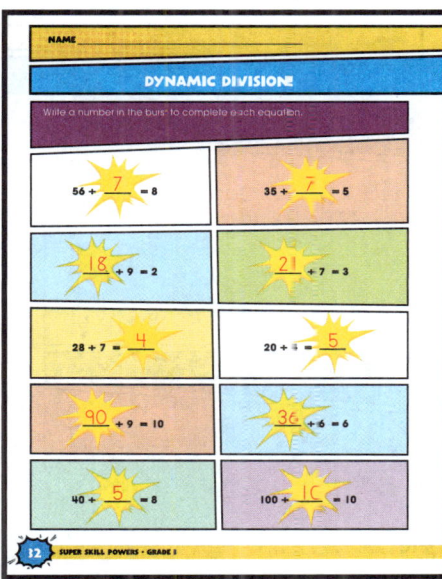
Page 32

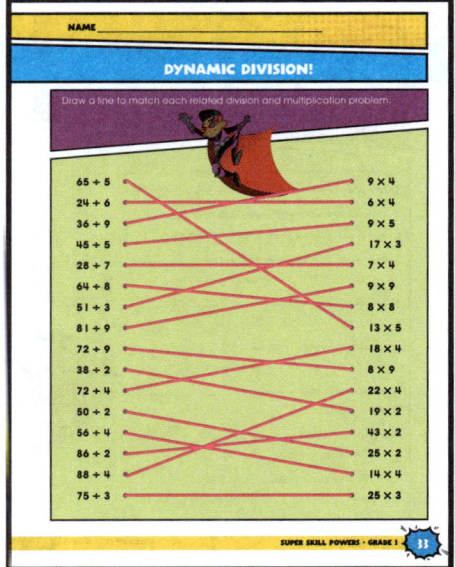
Page 33

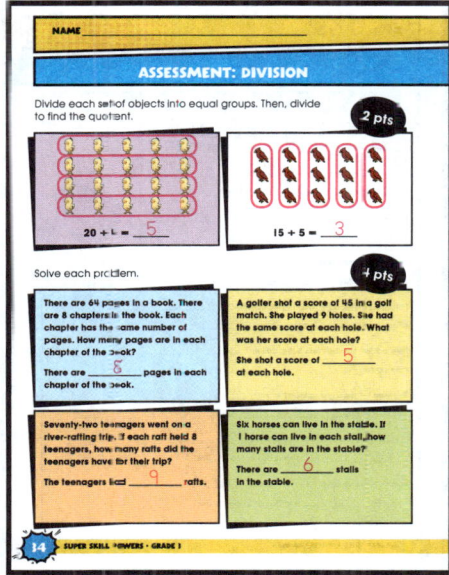
Page 34

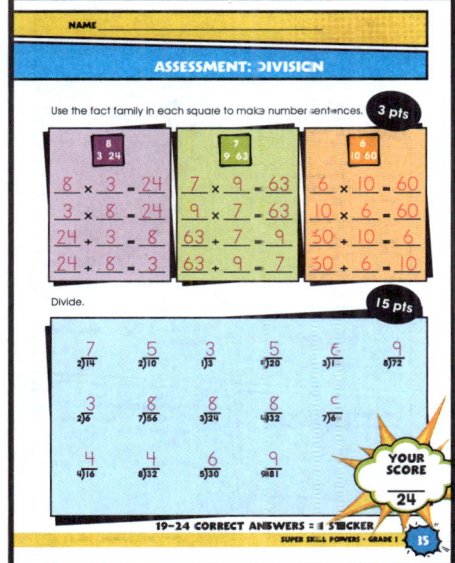
Page 35

ANSWER KEY

Page 40

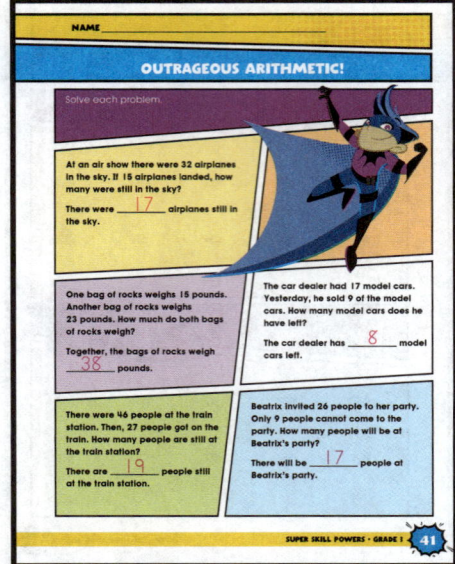

Page 41

Page 42

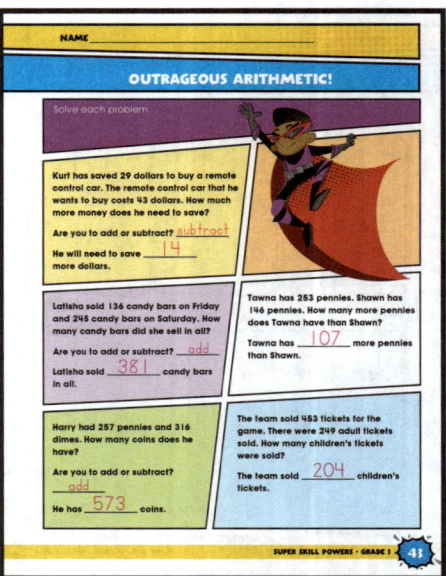

Page 43

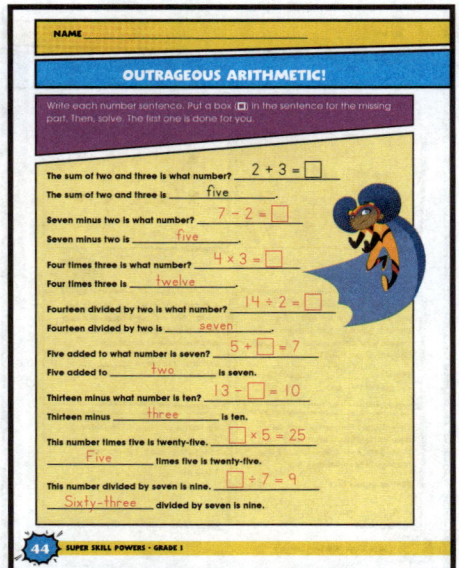

Page 44

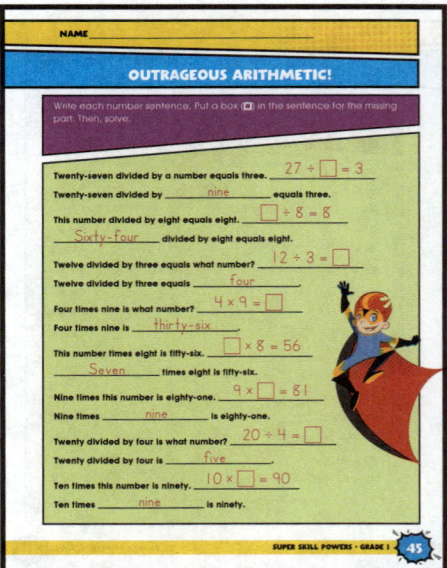

Page 45

ANSWER KEY

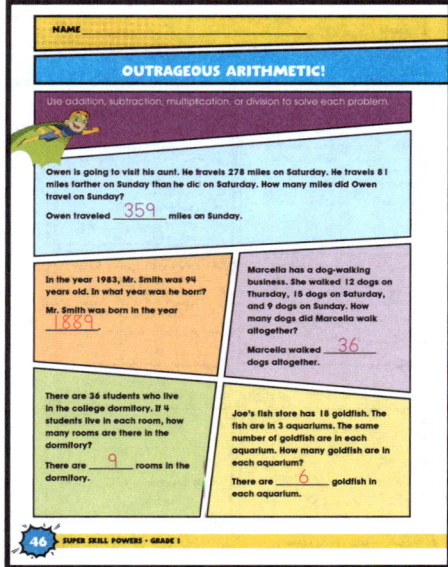
Page 46

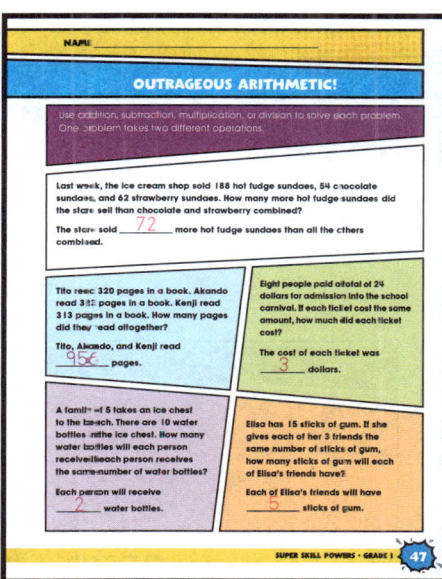
Page 47

Page 48

Page 49

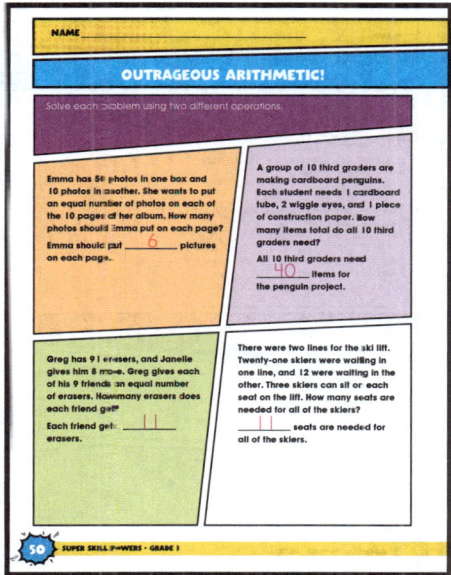
Page 50

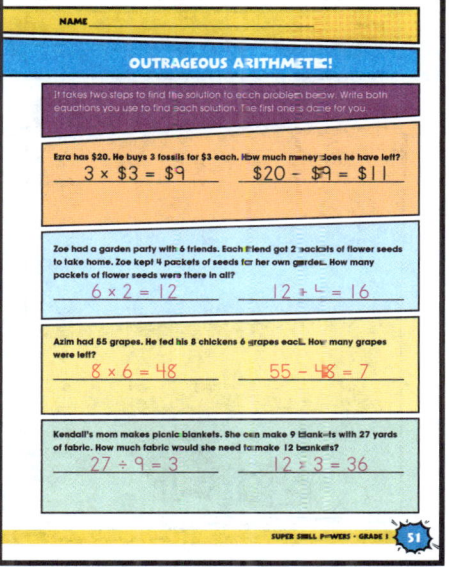
Page 51

ANSWER KEY

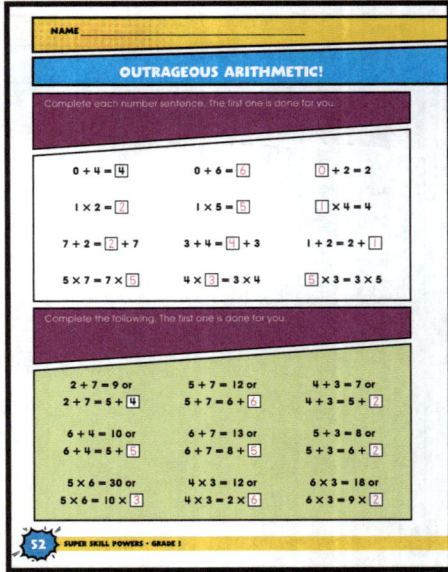
Page 52

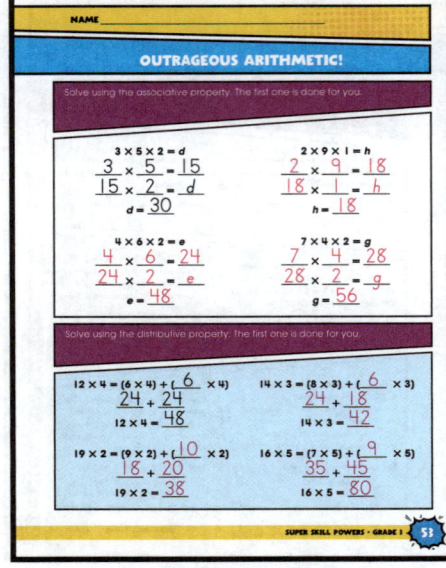
Page 53

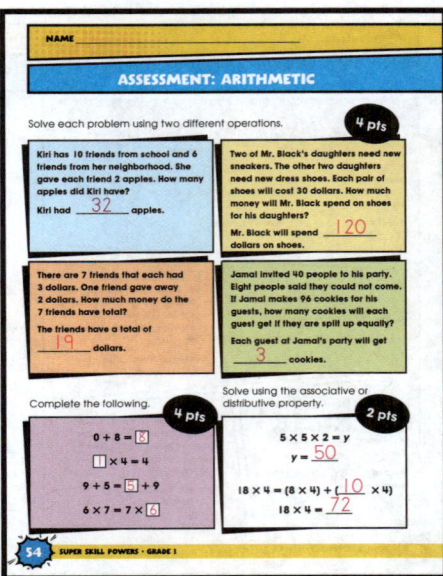
Page 54

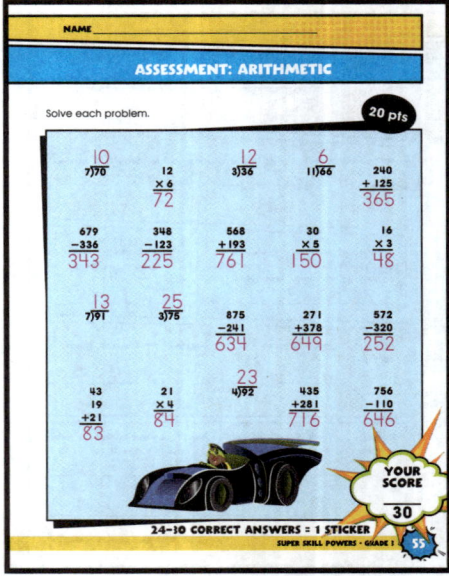
Page 55

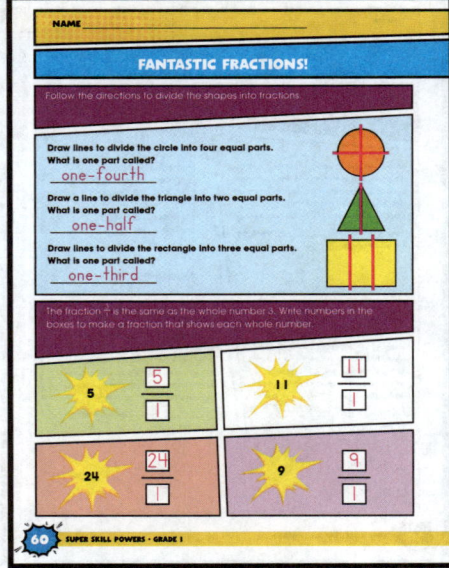
Page 60

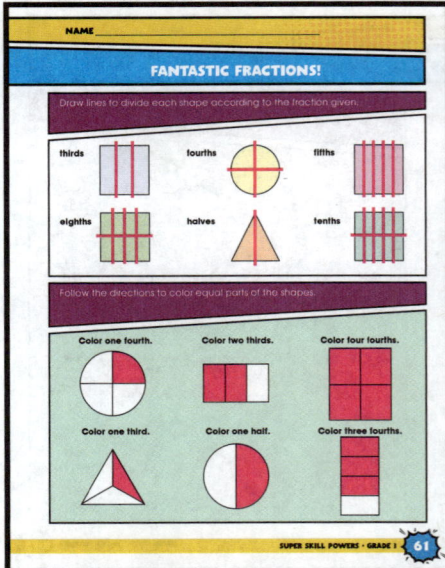
Page 61

ANSWER KEY

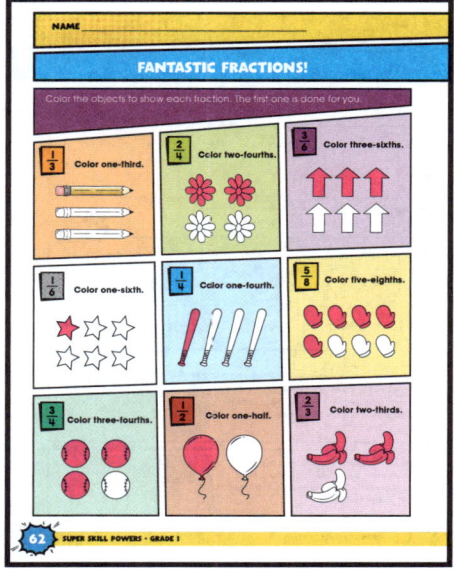

Page 62

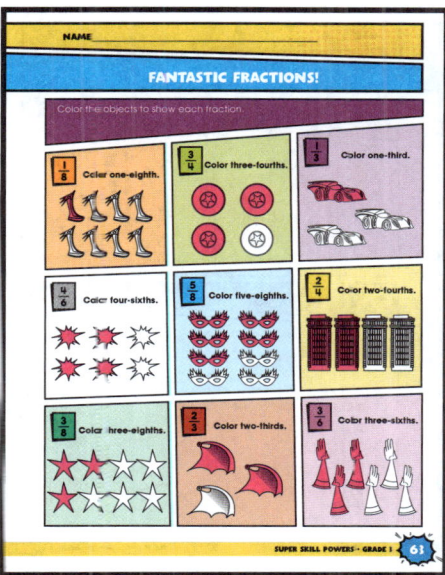

Page 63

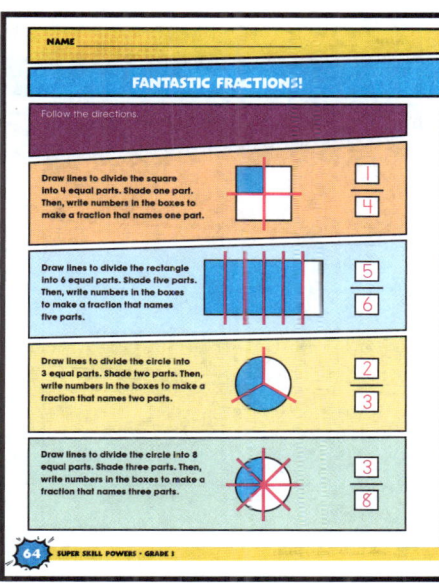

Page 64

Page 65

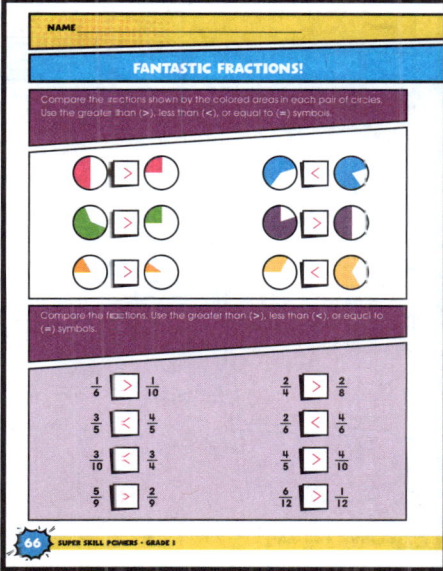

Page 66

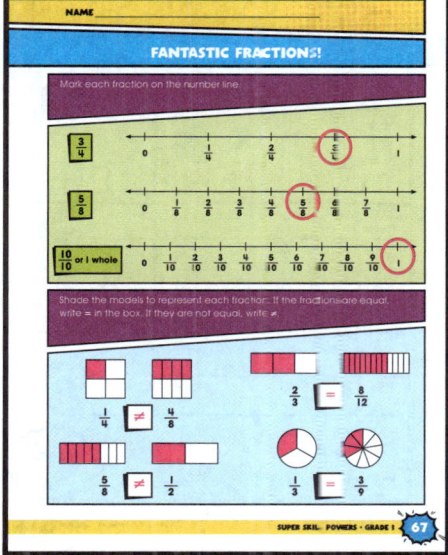

Page 67

ANSWER KEY

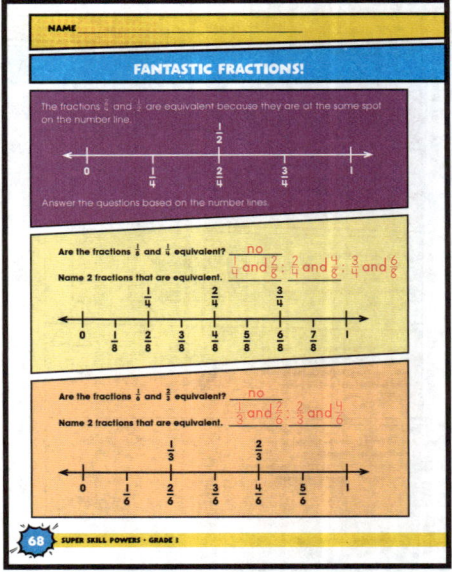
Page 68

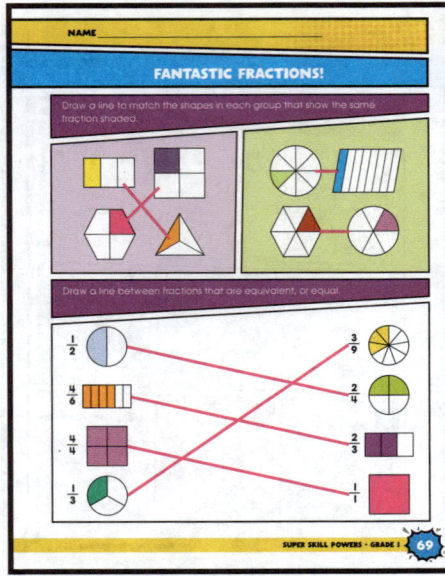
Page 69

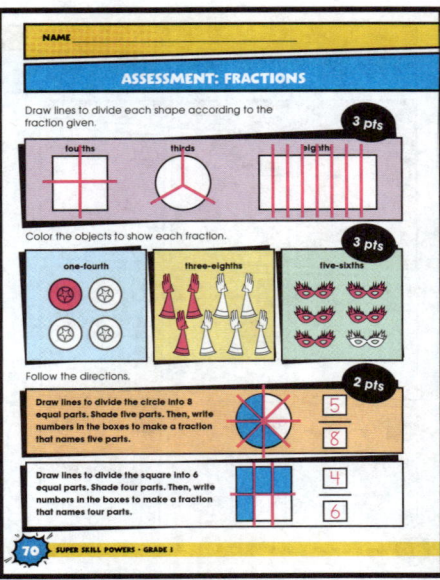
Page 70

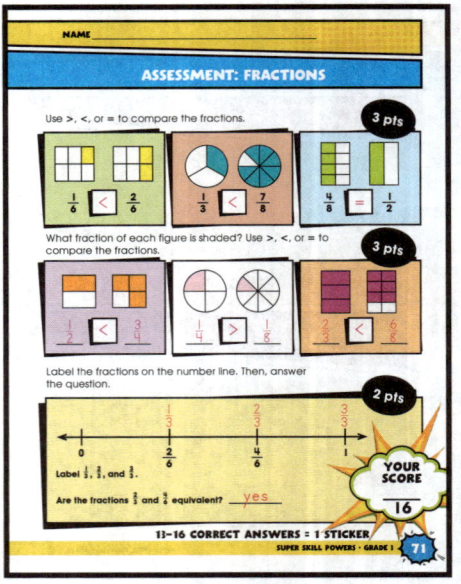
Page 71

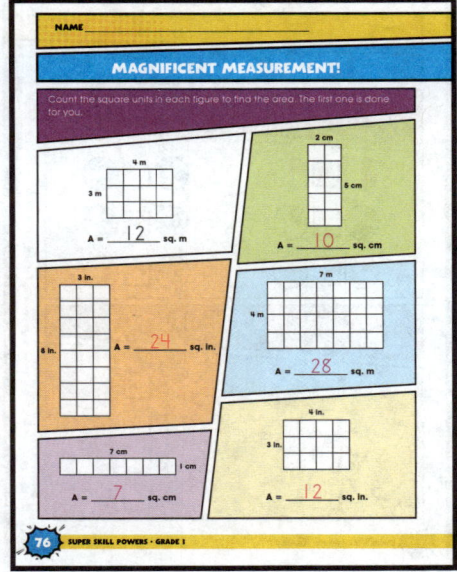
Page 76

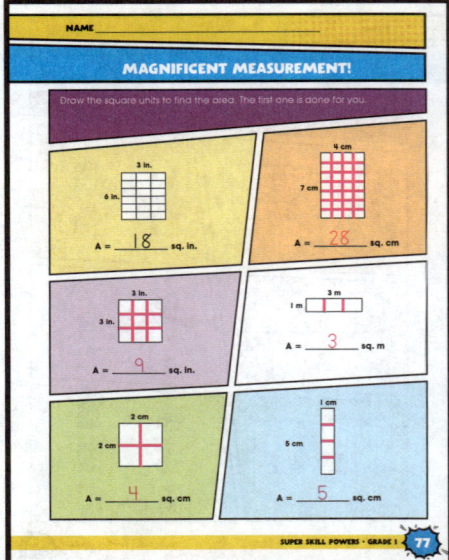
Page 77

ANSWER KEY

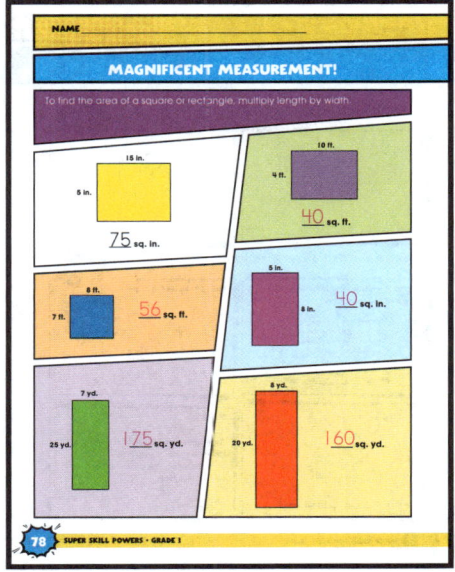
Page 78

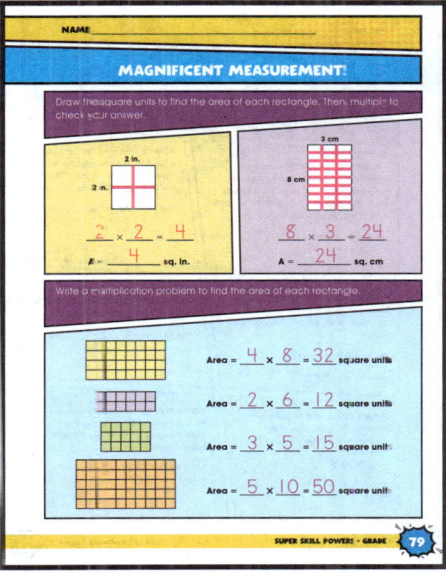
Page 79

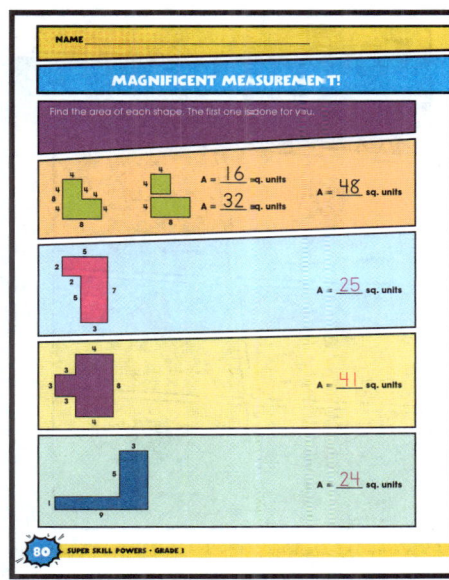
Page 80

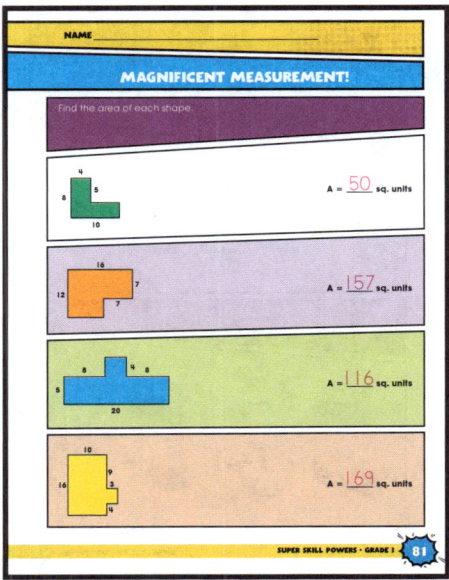
Page 81

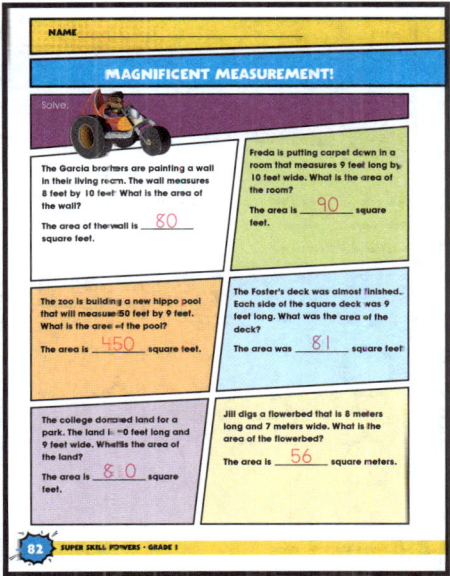
Page 82

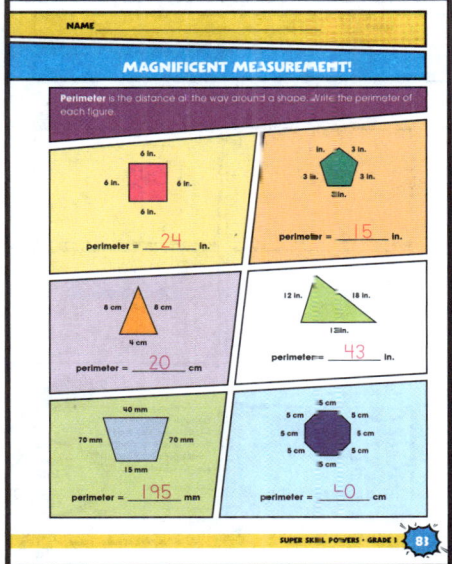
Page 83

ANSWER KEY

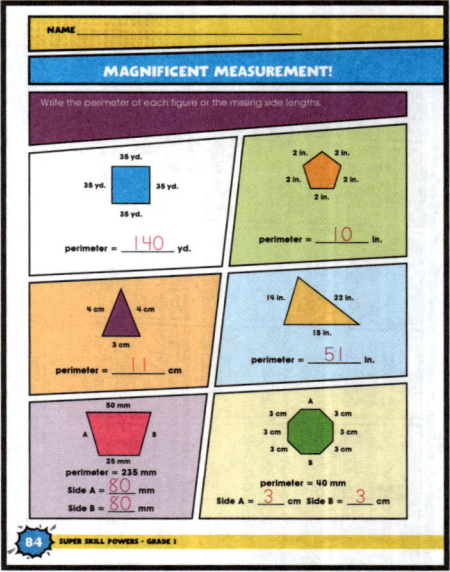
Page 84

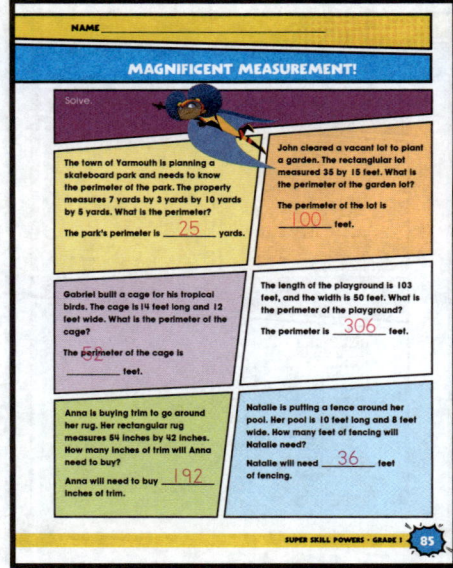
Page 85

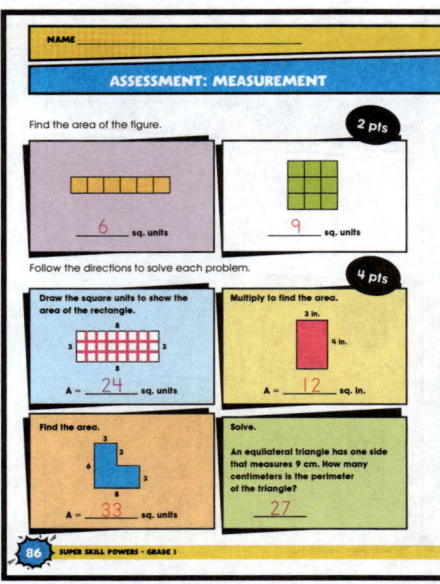
Page 86

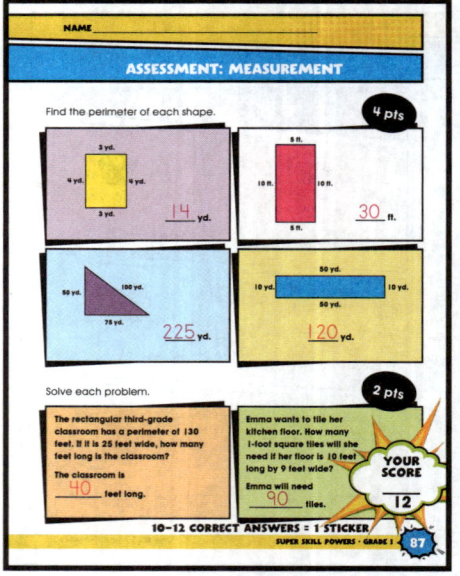
Page 87

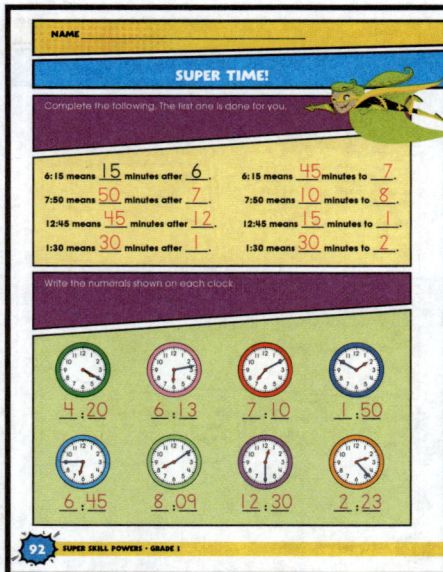
Page 92

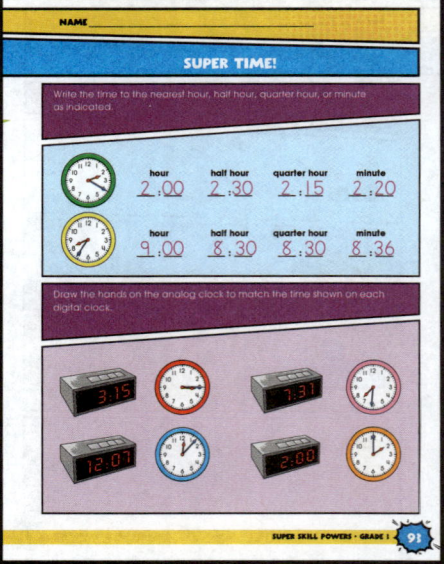
Page 93

ANSWER KEY

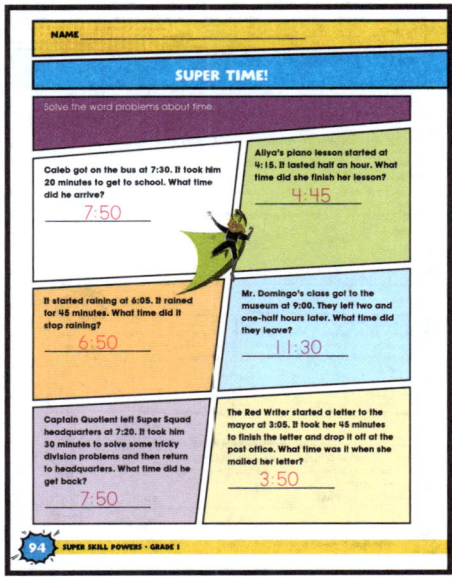
Page 94

Page 95

Page 96

Page 97

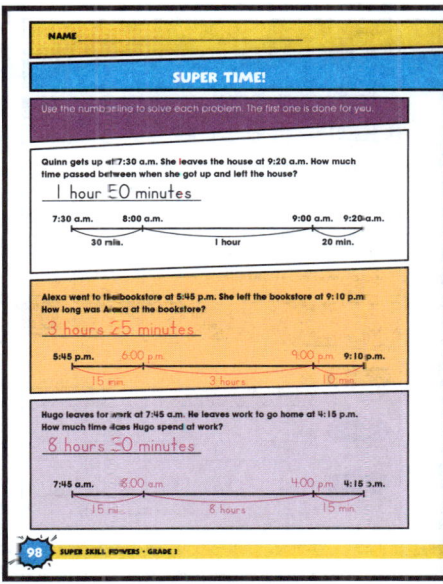
Page 98

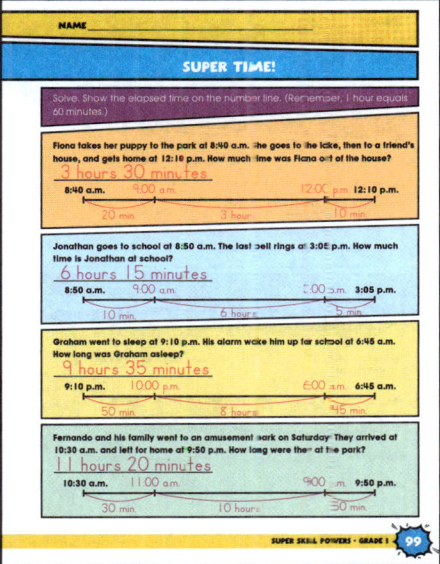
Page 99

ANSWER KEY

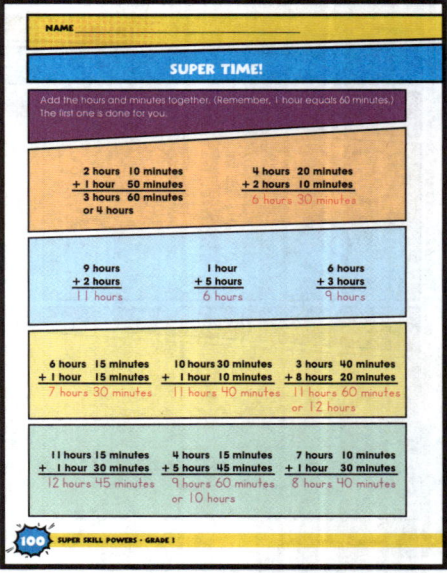

Page 100

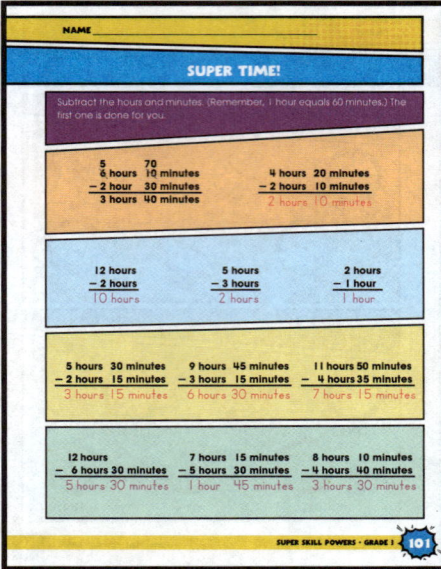

Page 101

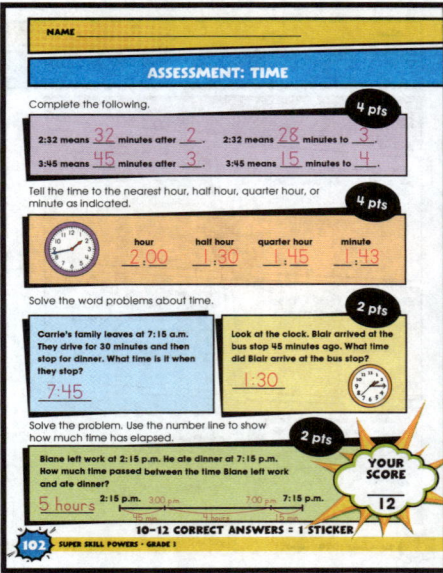

Page 102

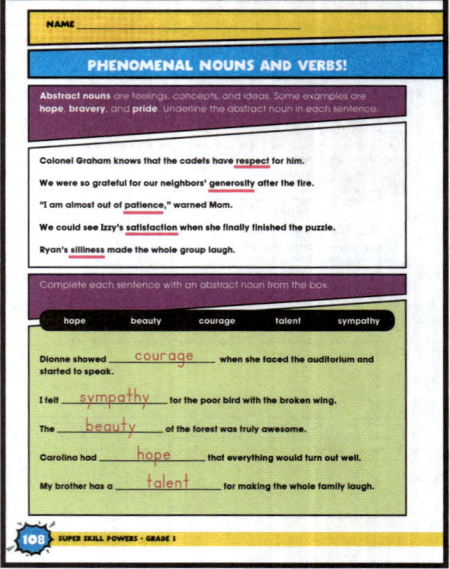

Page 108

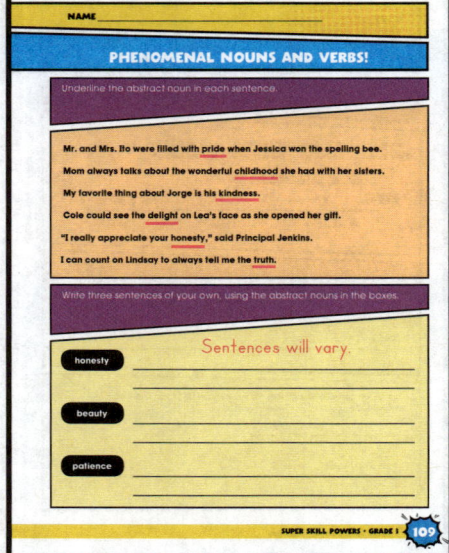

Page 109

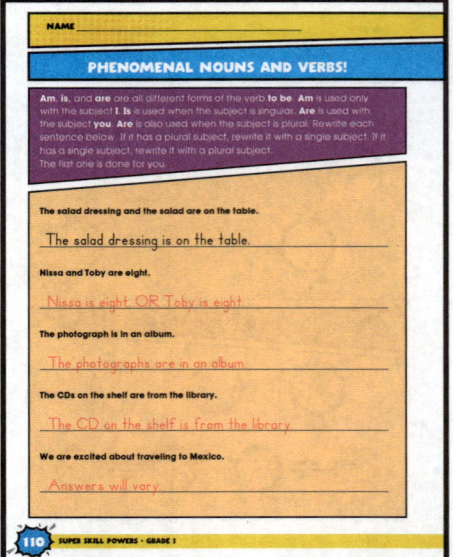

Page 110

ANSWER KEY

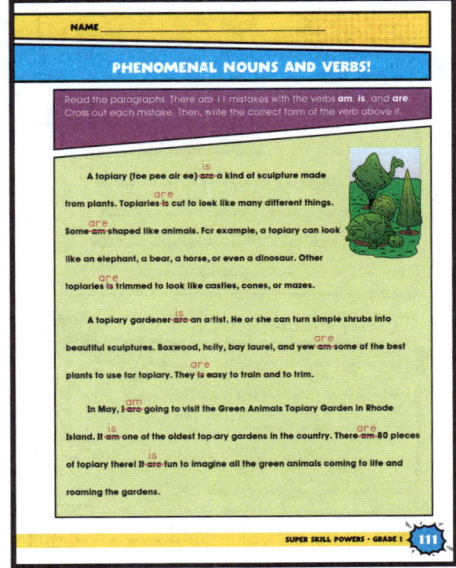

Page 111

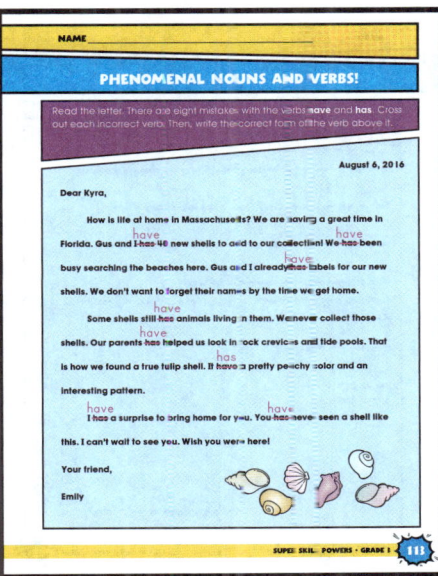

Page 112

Page 113

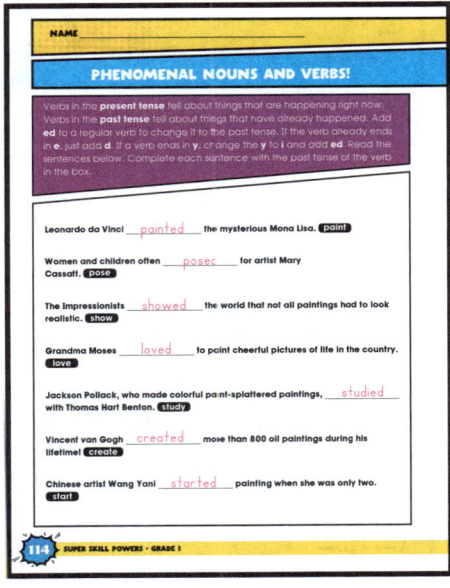

Page 114

Page 115

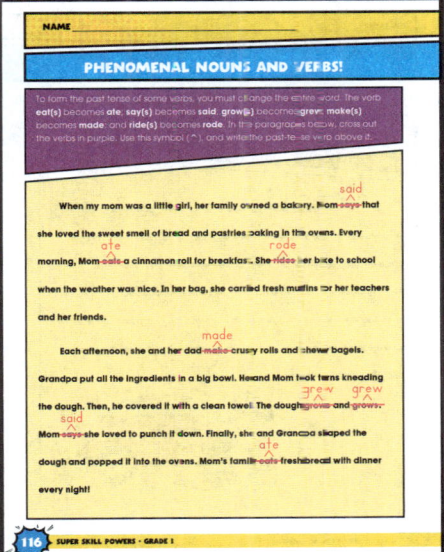

Page 116

ANSWER KEY

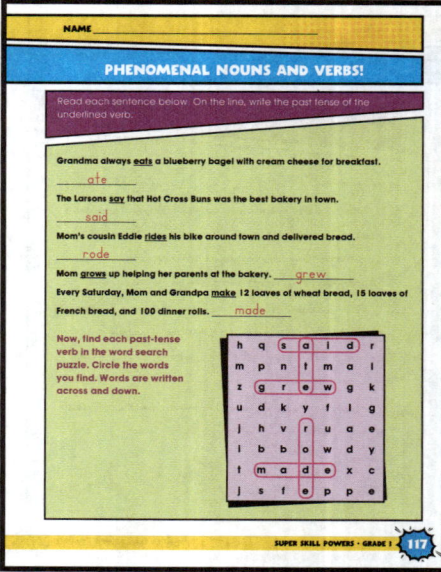

Page 117

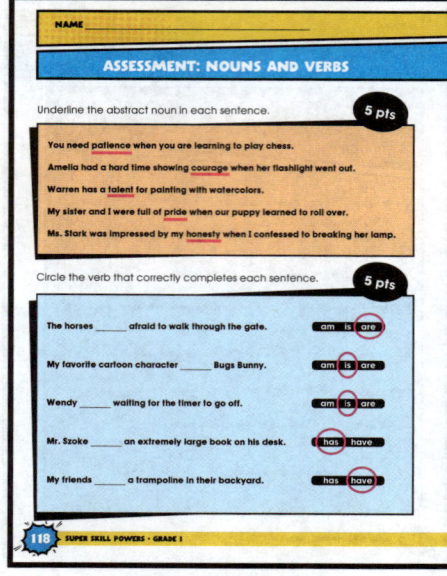

Page 118

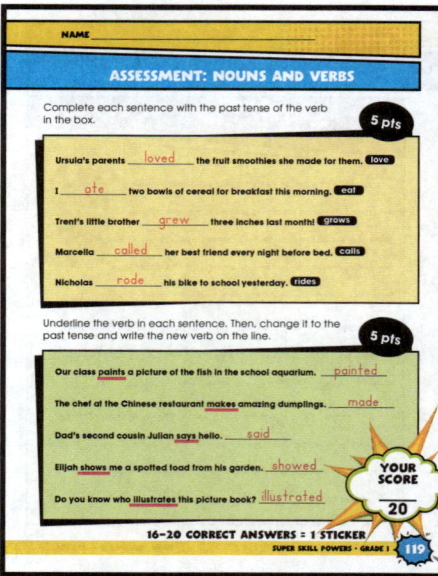

Page 119

Page 124

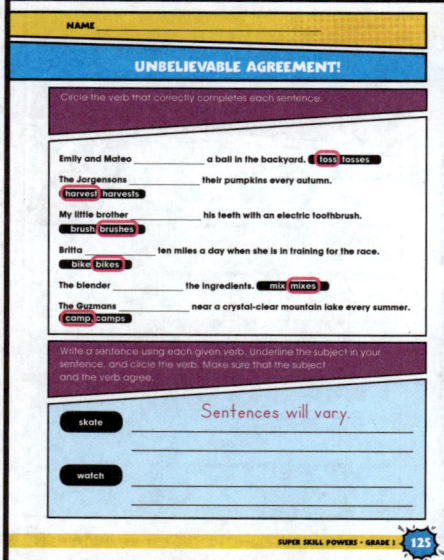

Page 125

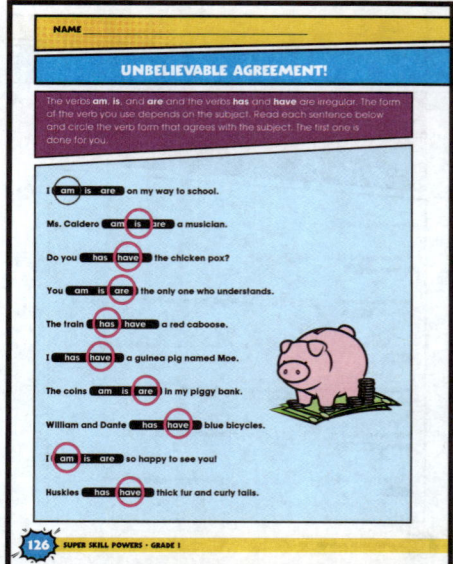

Page 126

ANSWER KEY

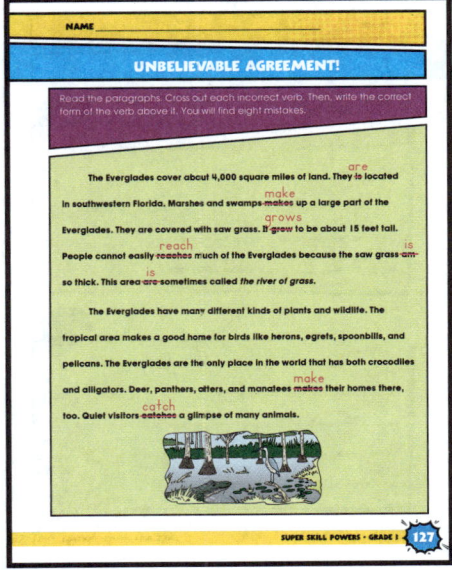

Page 127

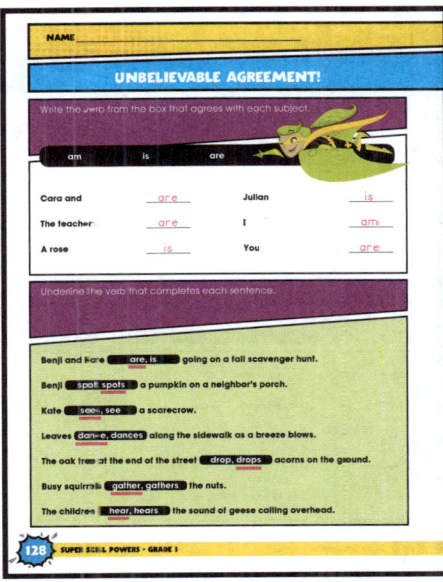

Page 128

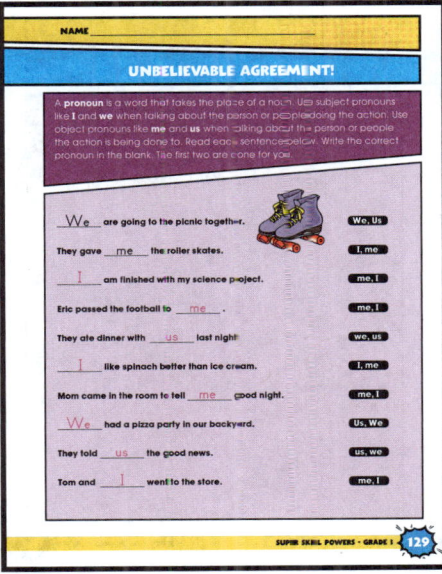

Page 129

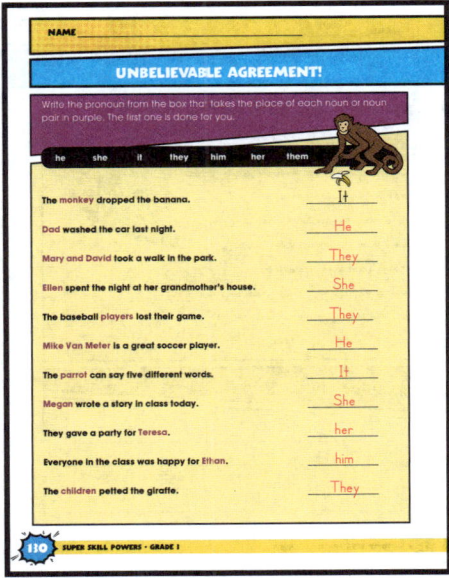

Page 130

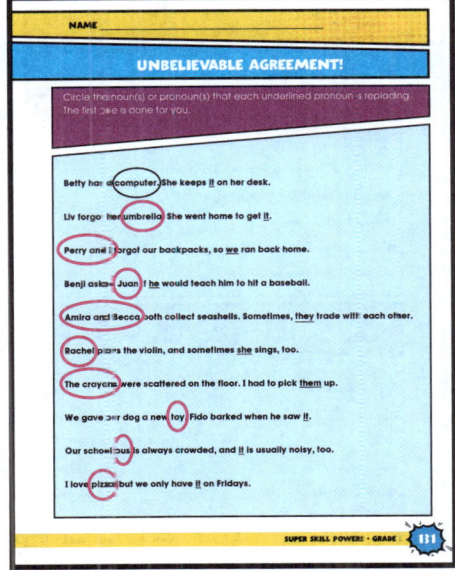

Page 131

Page 132

SUPER SKILL POWERS • GRADE 3   233

ANSWER KEY

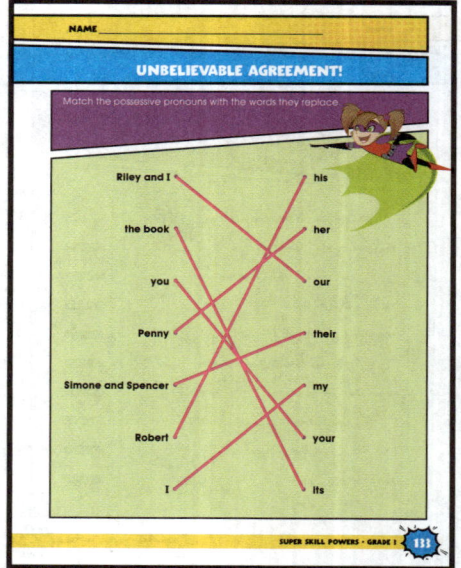

Page 133

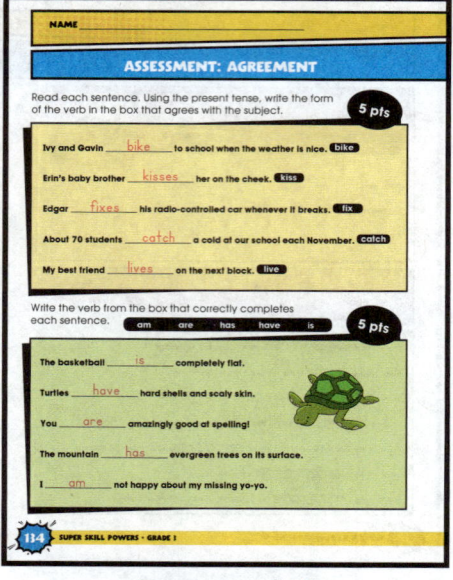

Page 134

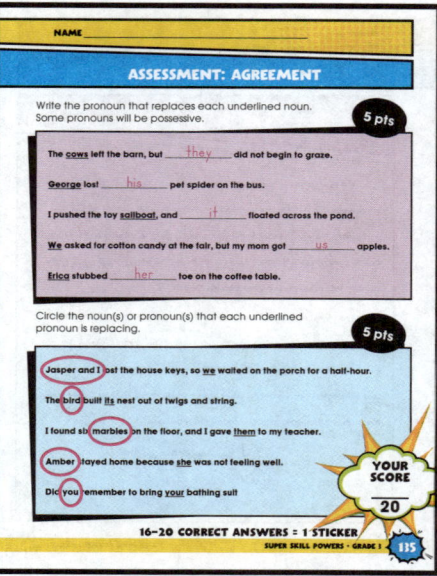

Page 135

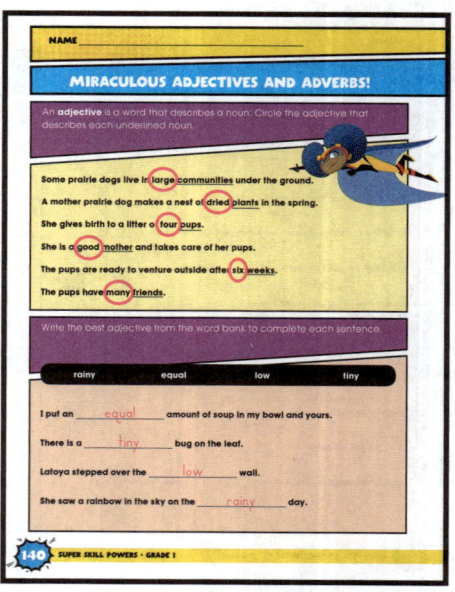

Page 140

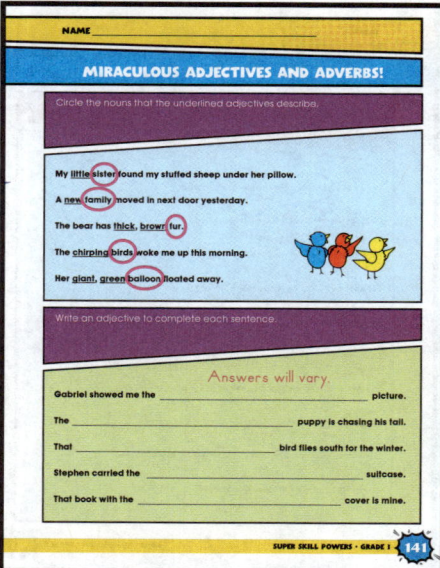

Page 141

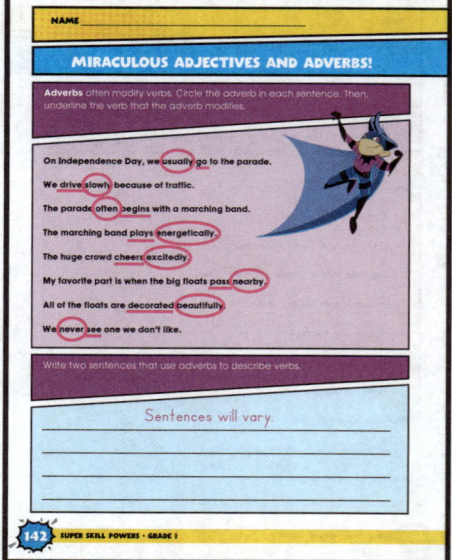

Page 142

ANSWER KEY

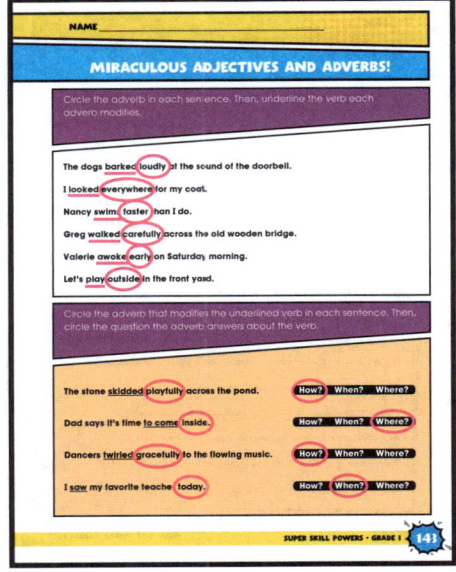
Page 143

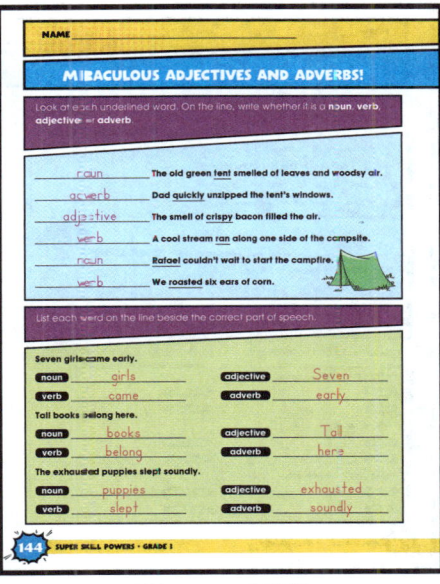
Page 144

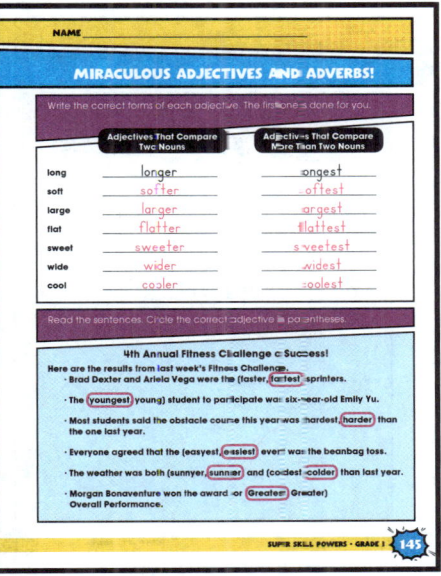
Page 145

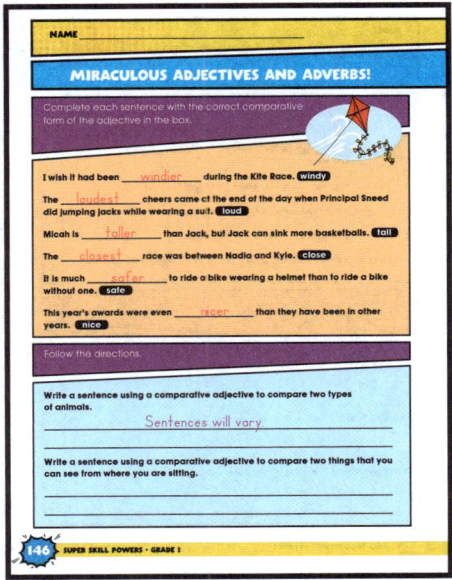
Page 146

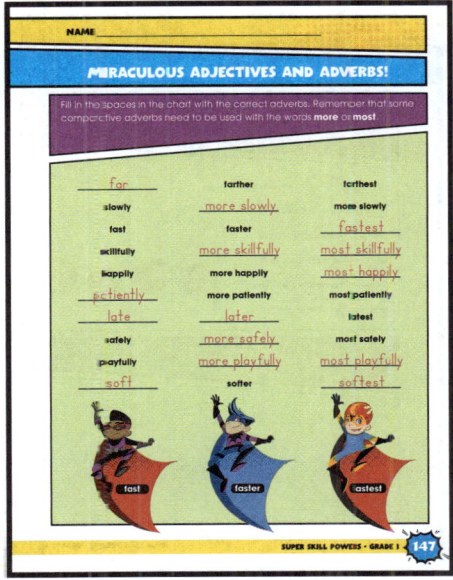
Page 147

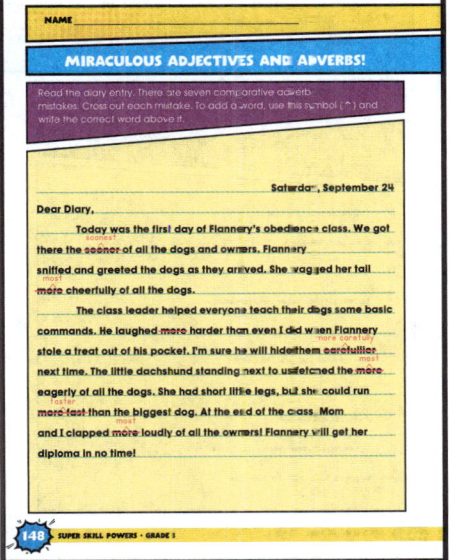
Page 148

ANSWER KEY

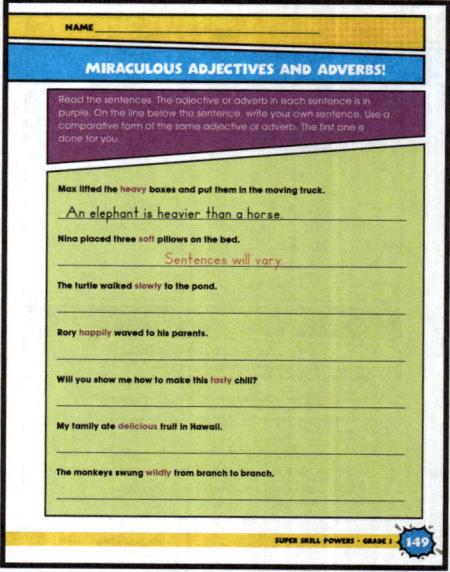

Page 149

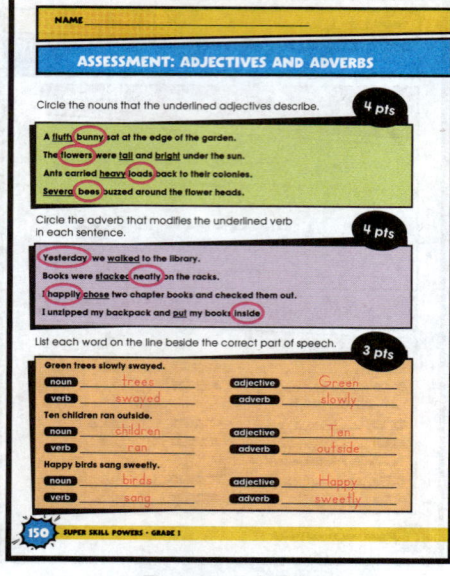

Page 150

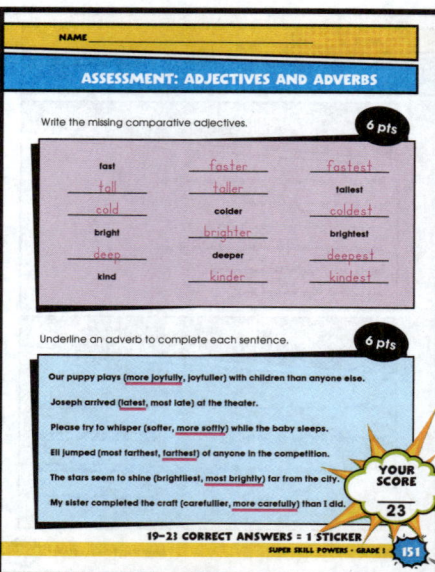

Page 151

Page 156

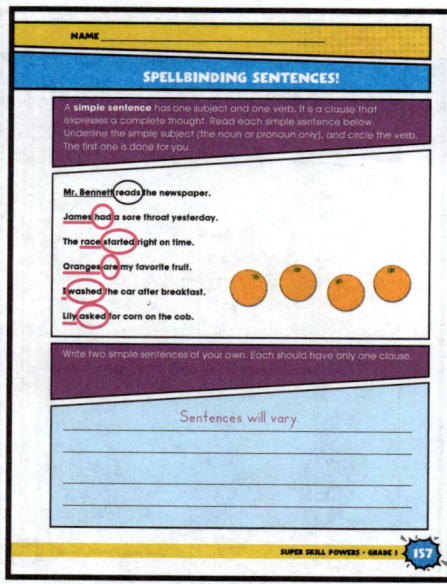

Page 157

Page 158

ANSWER KEY

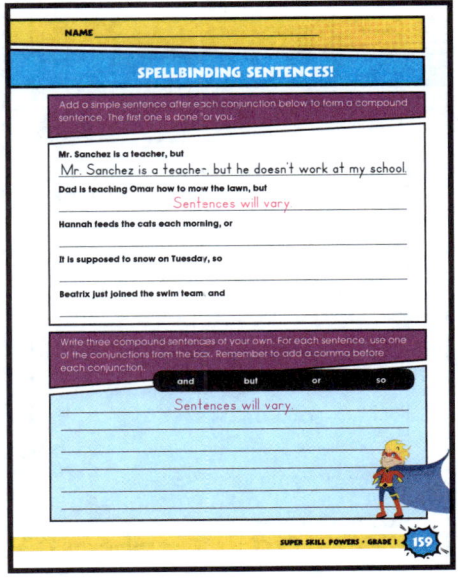
Page 159

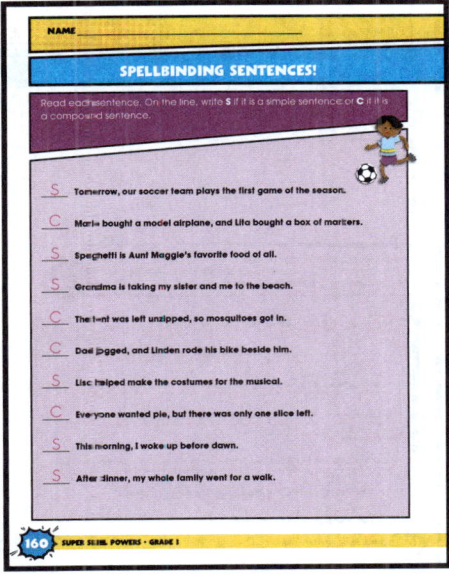
Page 160

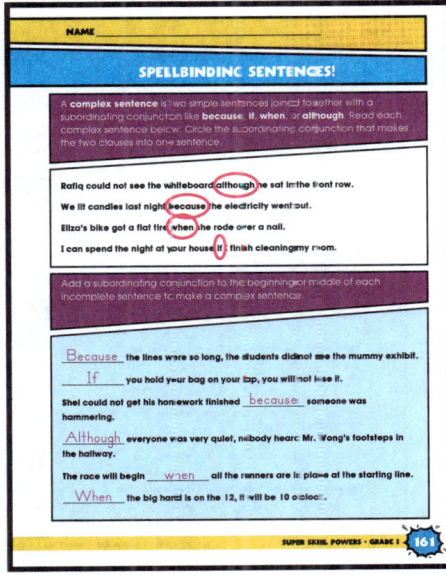
Page 161

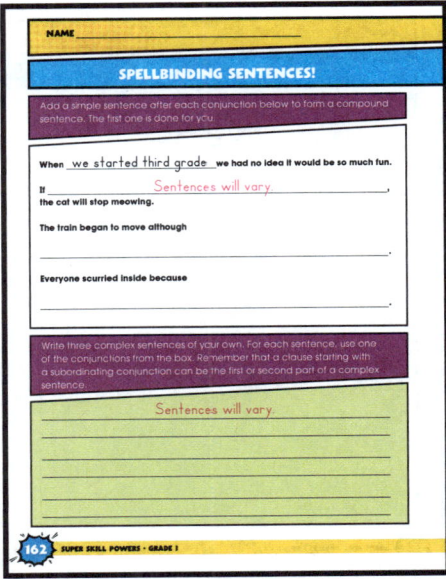
Page 162

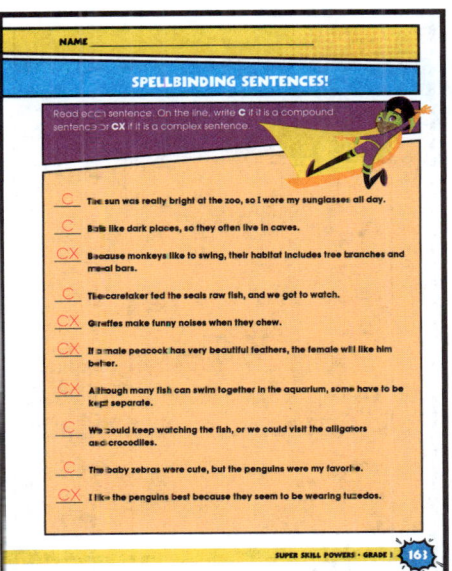
Page 163

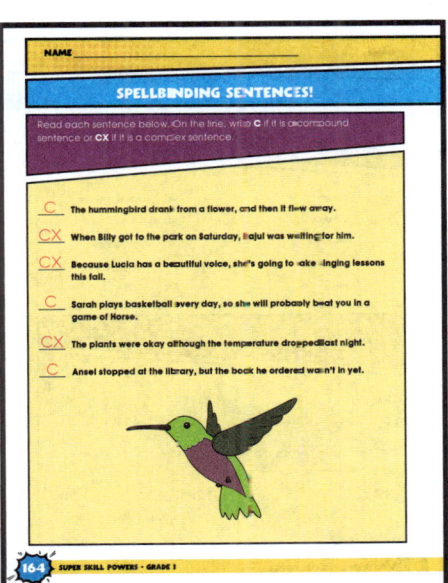
Page 164

ANSWER KEY

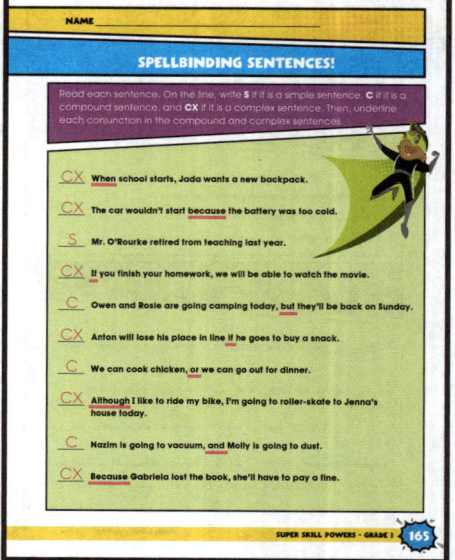

Page 165

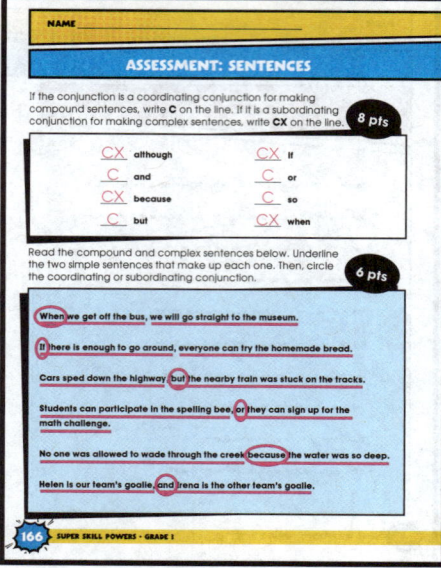

Page 166

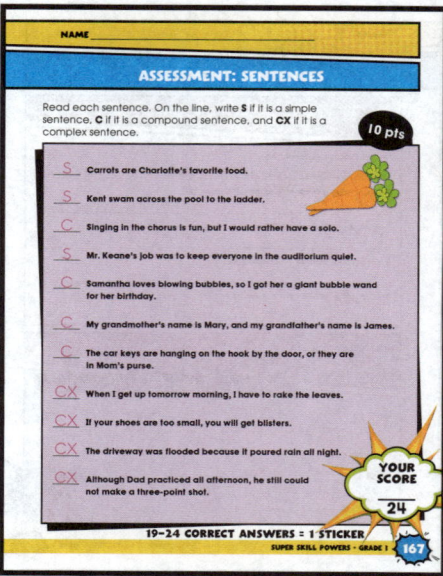

Page 167

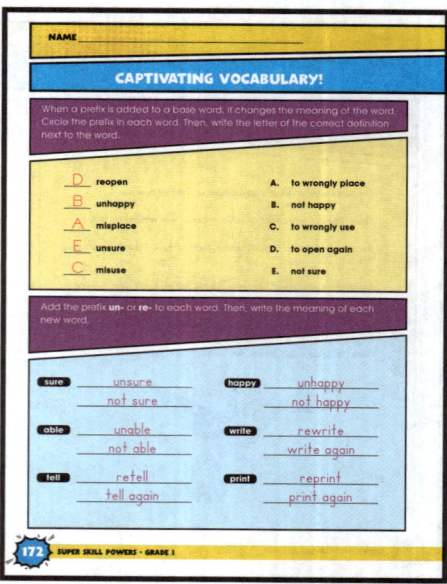

Page 172

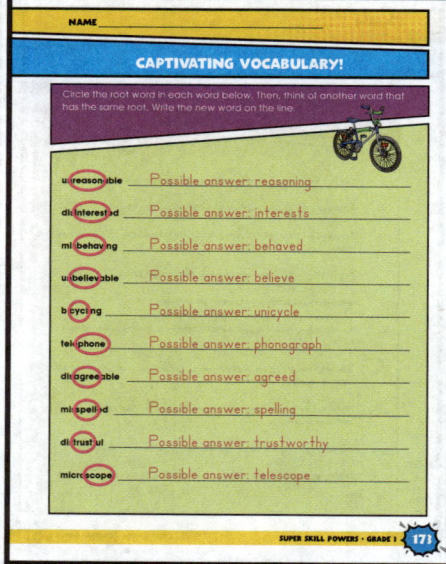

Page 173

Page 174

ANSWER KEY

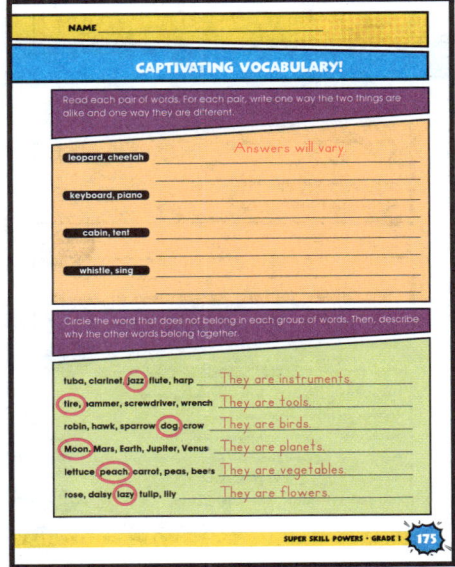
Page 175

Page 176

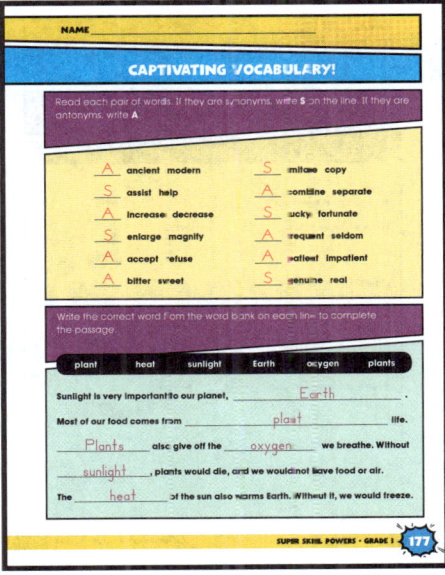
Page 177

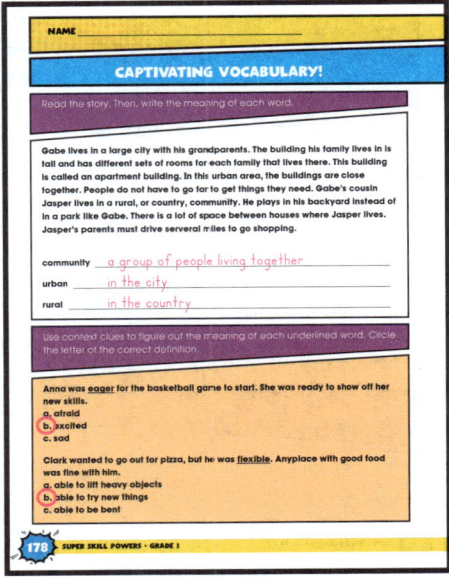
Page 178

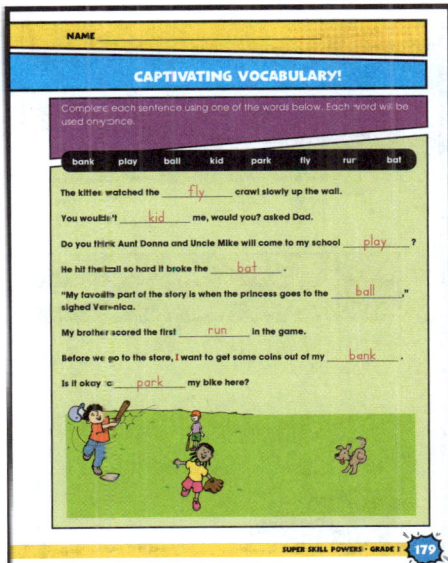
Page 179

Page 180

ANSWER KEY

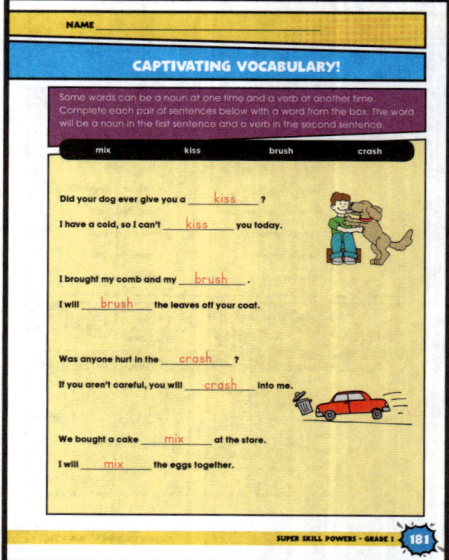

Page 181

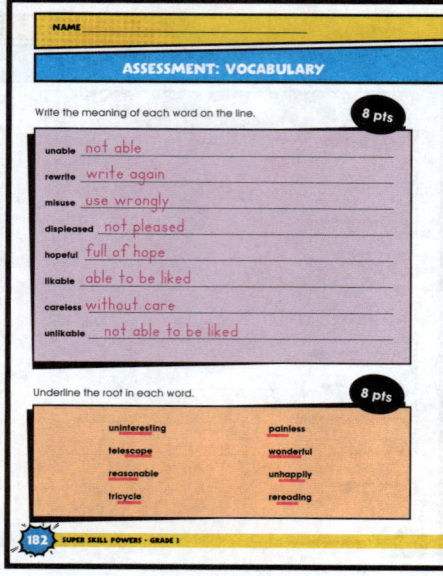

Page 182

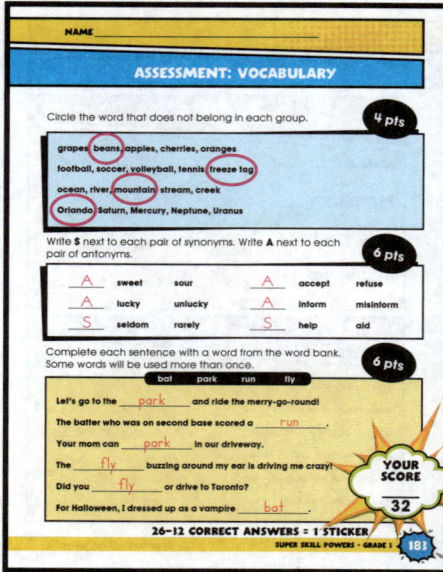

Page 183

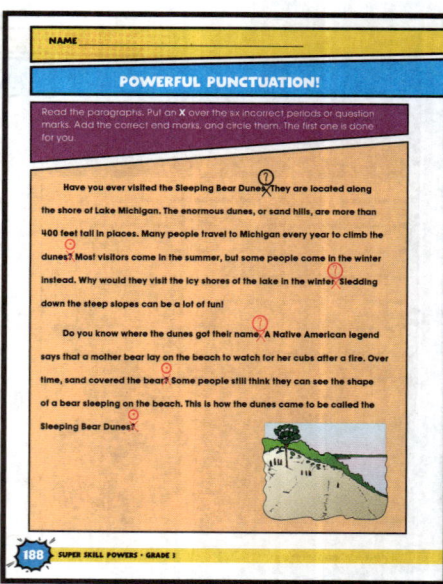

Page 188

Page 189

Page 190

SUPER SKILL POWERS • GRADE 3

ANSWER KEY

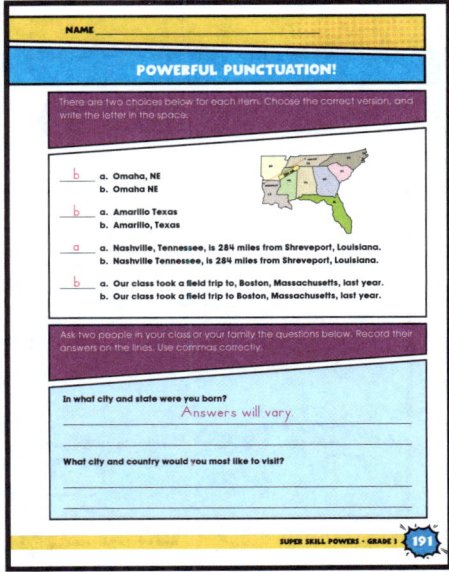
Page 191

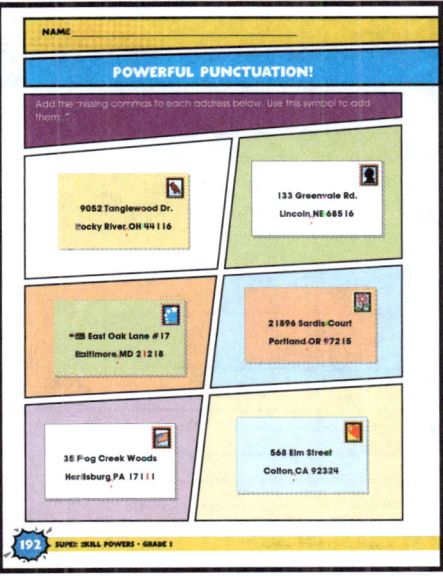
Page 192

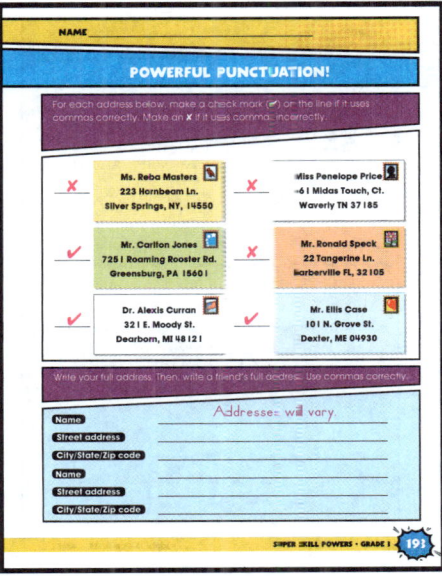
Page 193

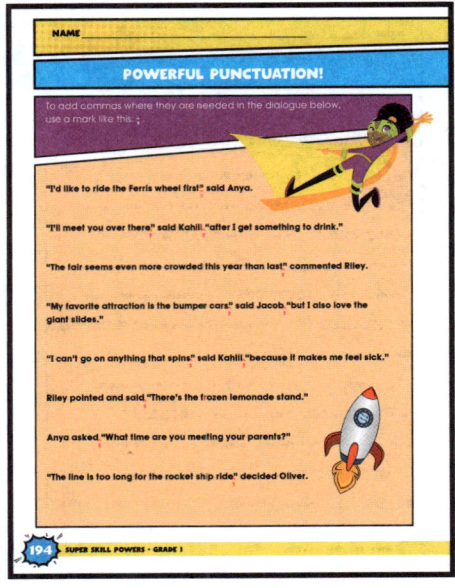
Page 194

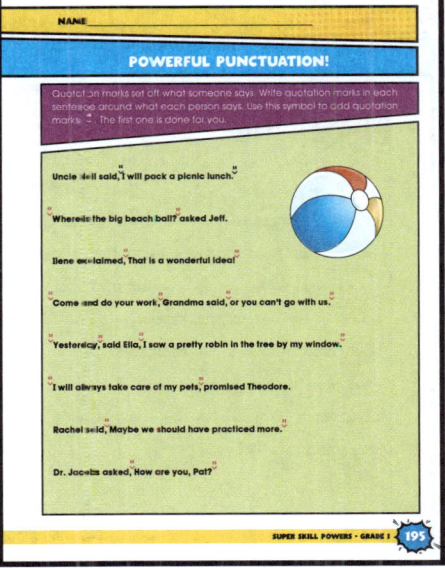
Page 195

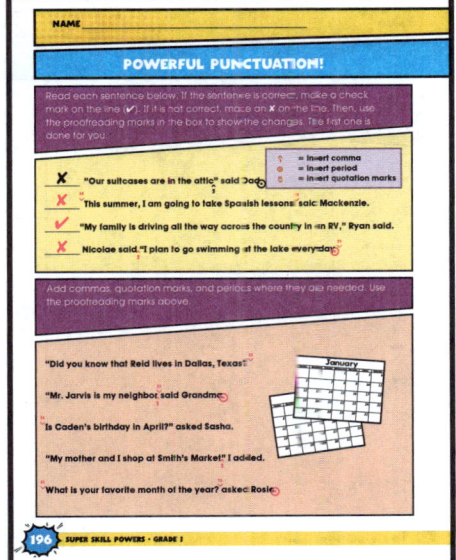
Page 196

ANSWER KEY

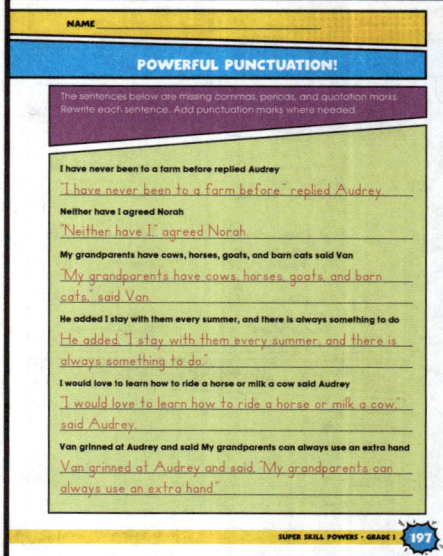
Page 197

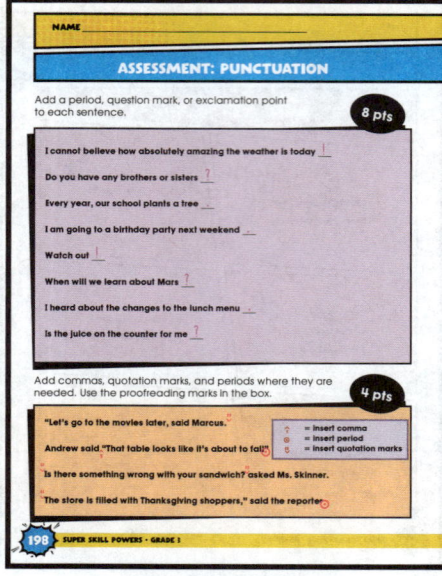
Page 198

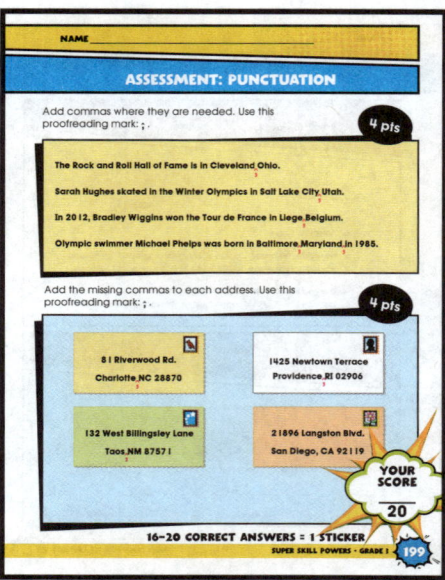
Page 199

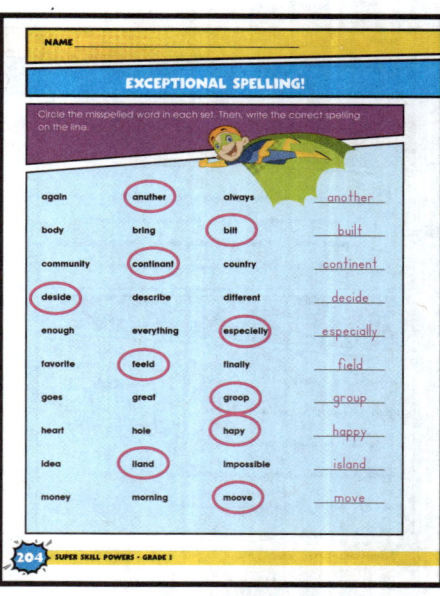
Page 204

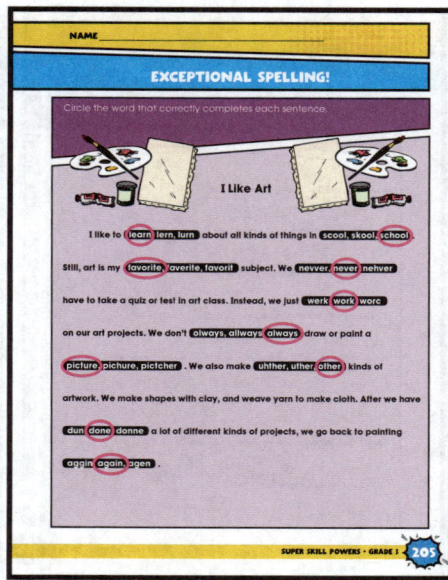
Page 205

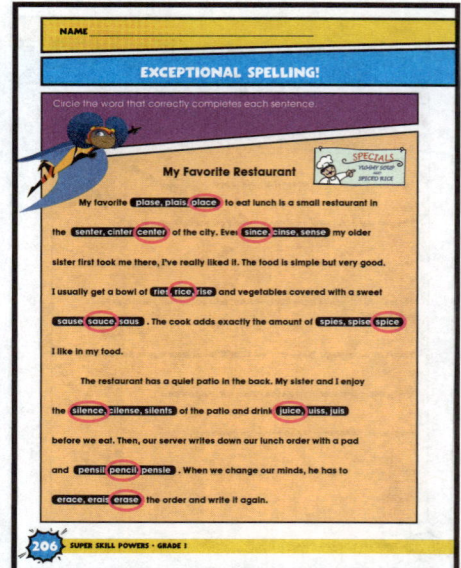
Page 206

ANSWER KEY

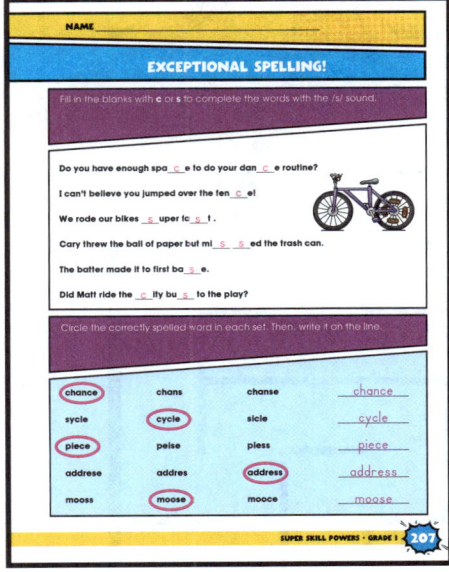
Page 207

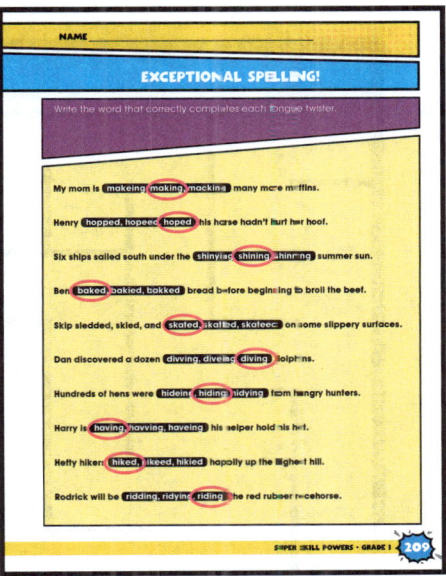
Page 208

Page 209

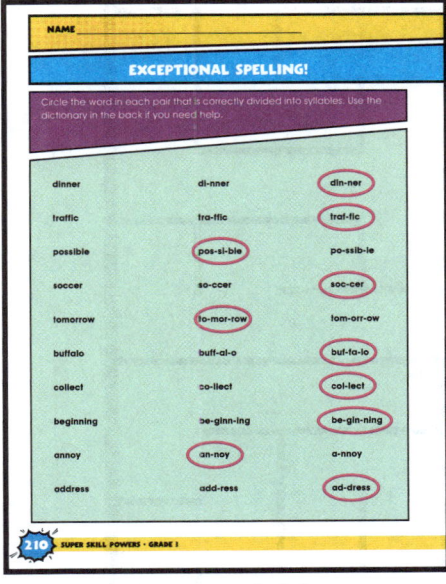
Page 210

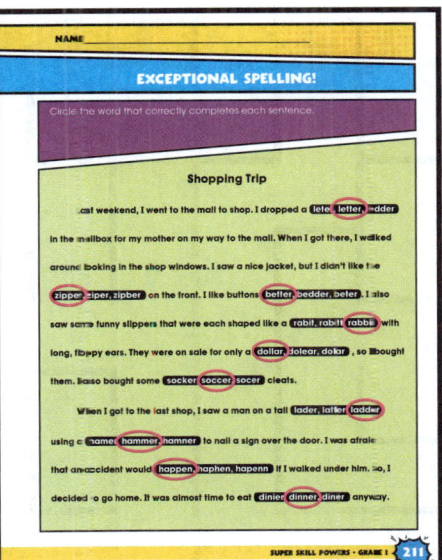
Page 211

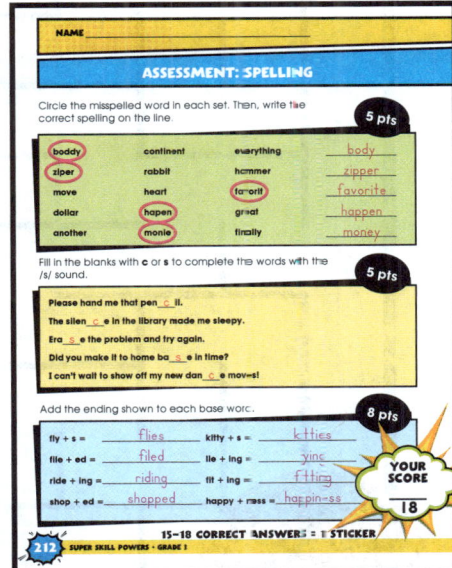
Page 212

NAME _____

BONUS ACTIVITY

Help the superhero find his shield.

Start

Finish

244 SUPER SKILL POWERS • GRADE 3

BONUS ACTIVITY

Help the superhero win the race.

Finish

Start

SUPER SKILL POWERS • GRADE 3

BONUS ACTIVITY

Help the superhero escape from the volcano.

Start

Finish

NAME _____

BONUS ACTIVITY

Help the superhero reach the ship in time.

Finish

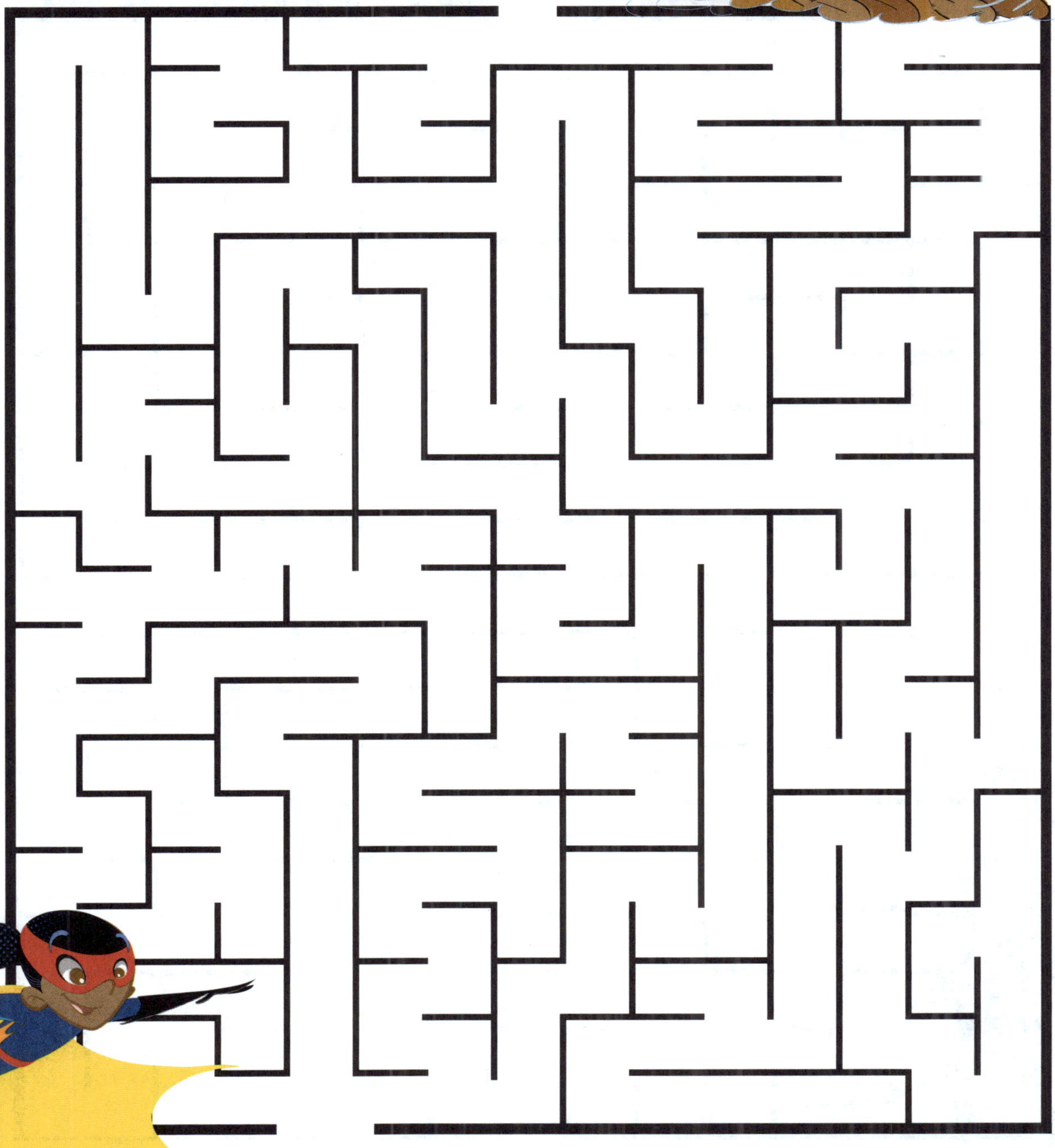

Start

SUPER SKILL POWERS • GRADE 3   247

NAME

BONUS ACTIVITY

Help the superhero save the city.

BONUS ACTIVITY

Solve each problem. Then, connect the dots to finish the picture, starting at the lowest product.

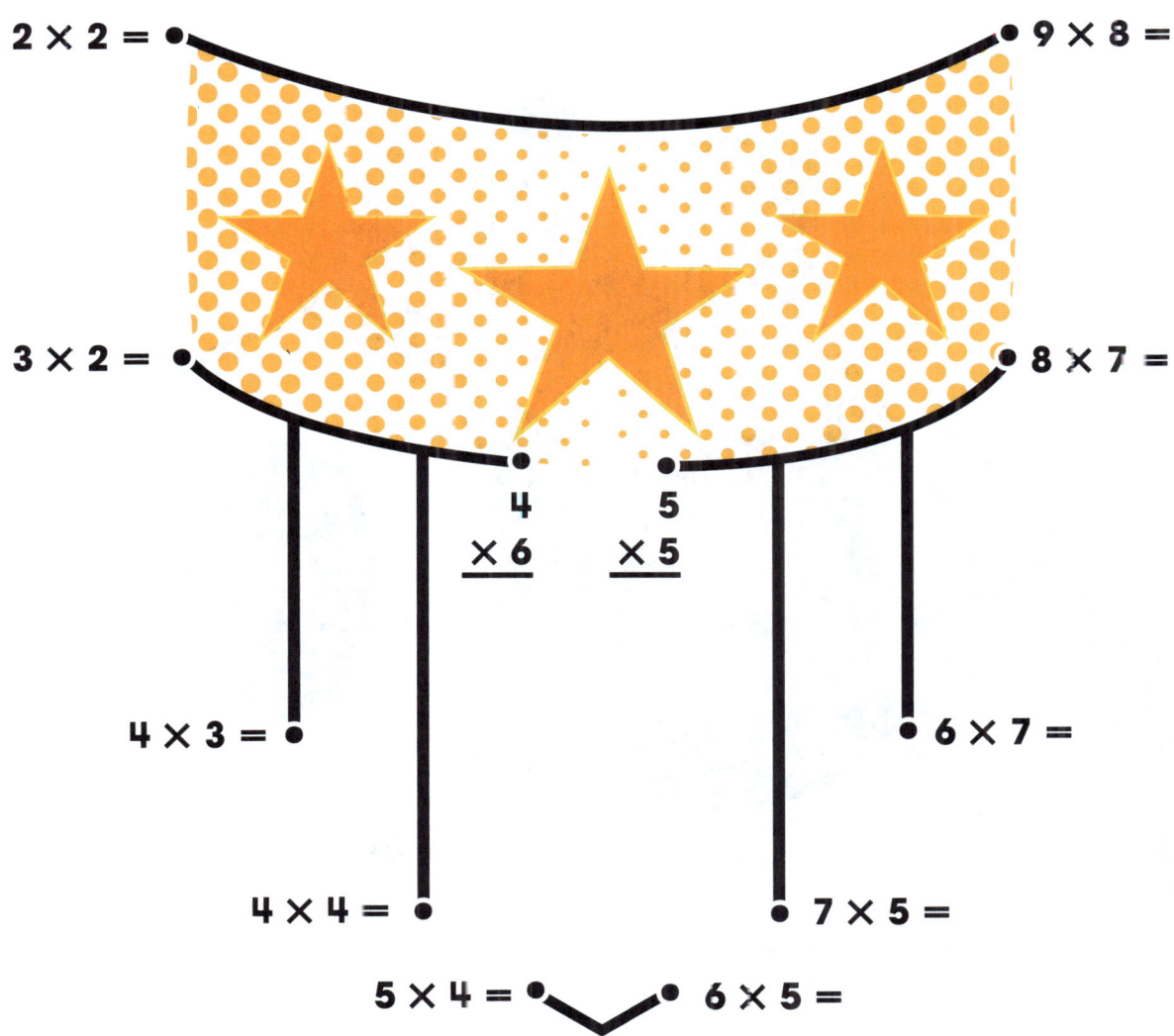

2 × 2 =

9 × 8 =

3 × 2 =

8 × 7 =

4
×6

5
×5

4 × 3 =

6 × 7 =

4 × 4 =

7 × 5 =

5 × 4 =

6 × 5 =

BONUS ACTIVITY

NAME _____

Solve each problem. Then, connect the two sets of dots to finish the picture, starting at the lowest quotient each time.

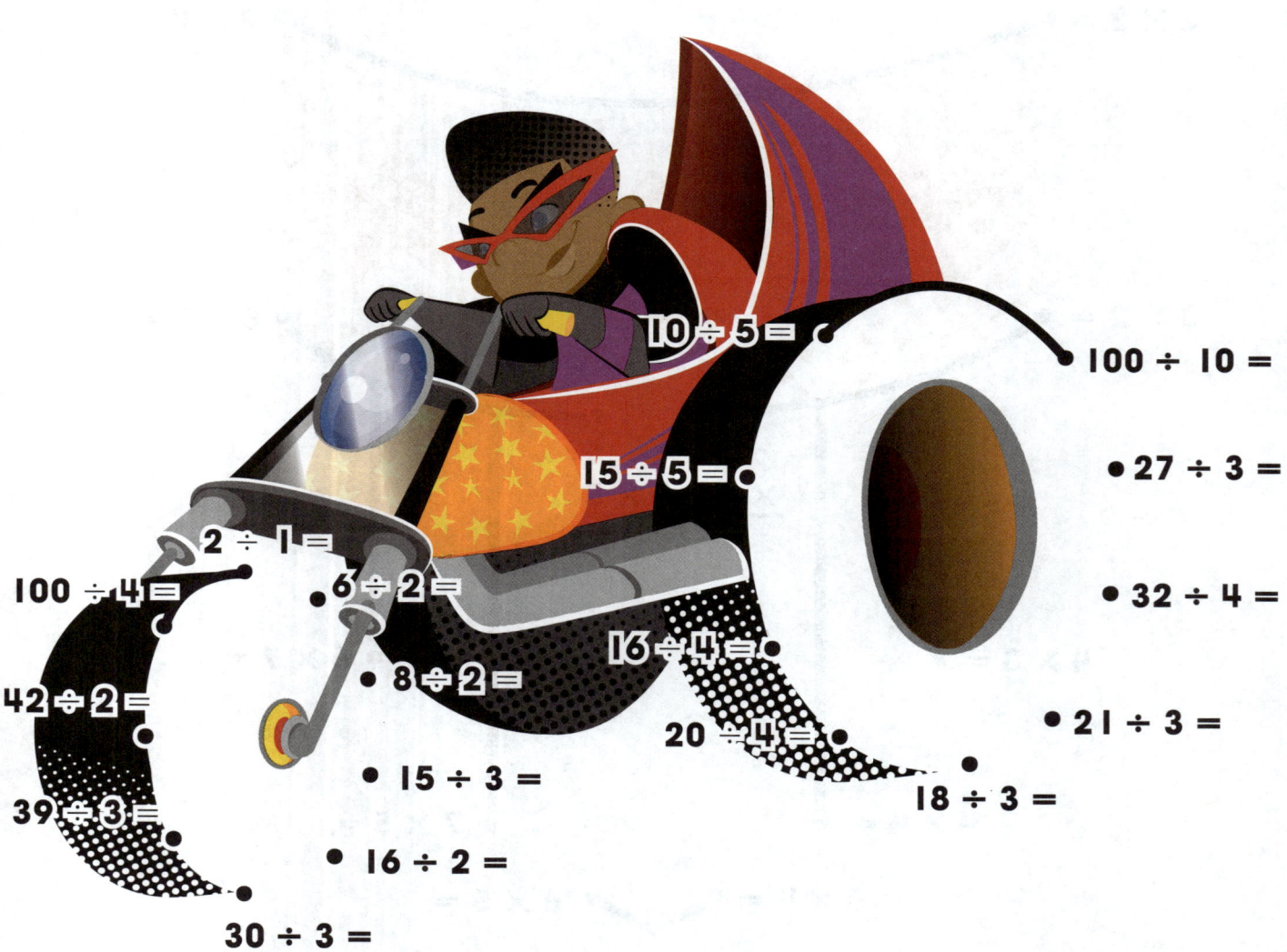

- 10 ÷ 5 =
- 100 ÷ 10 =
- 27 ÷ 3 =
- 15 ÷ 5 =
- 2 ÷ 1 =
- 100 ÷ 4 =
- 6 ÷ 2 =
- 32 ÷ 4 =
- 42 ÷ 2 =
- 8 ÷ 2 =
- 16 ÷ 4 =
- 21 ÷ 3 =
- 20 ÷ 4 =
- 39 ÷ 3 =
- 15 ÷ 3 =
- 18 ÷ 3 =
- 16 ÷ 2 =
- 30 ÷ 3 =

NAME _____

BONUS ACTIVITY

Solve each problem. Then, connect the dots to finish the picture, starting at the lowest solution. Include numbers that are provided.

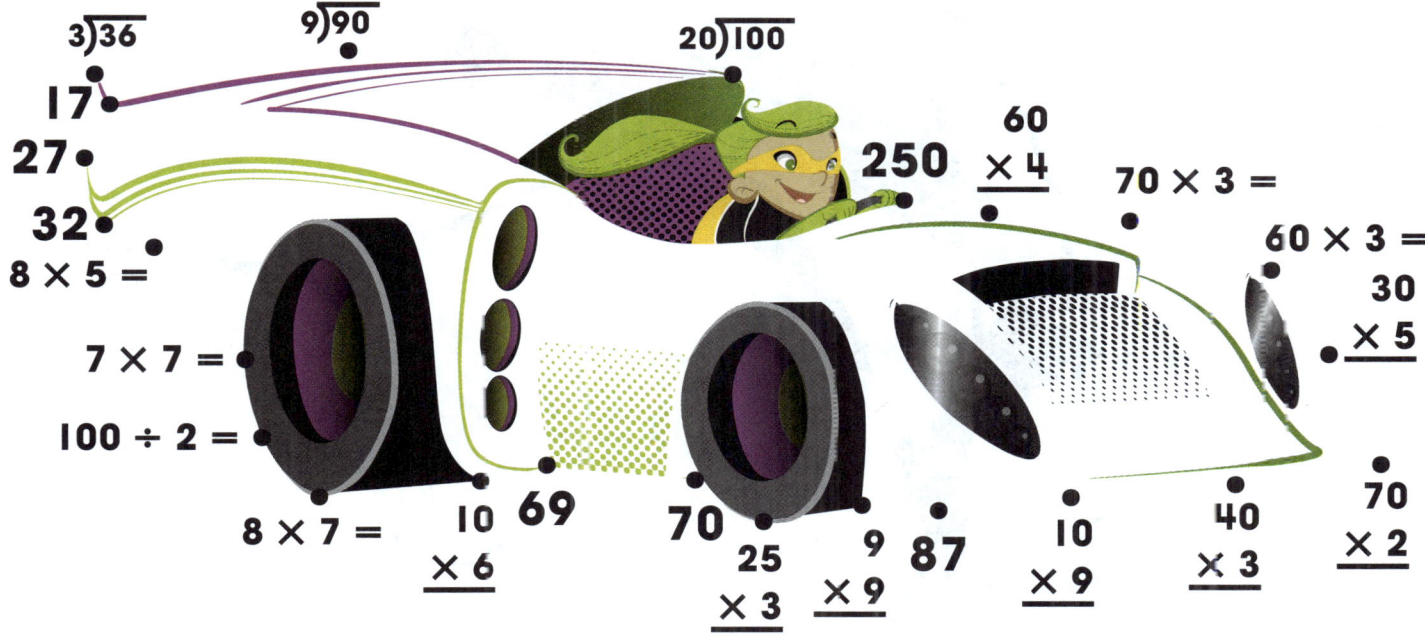

NAME _____

BONUS ACTIVITY

Solve each problem. Then, connect the dots to finish the picture, starting at the lowest difference.

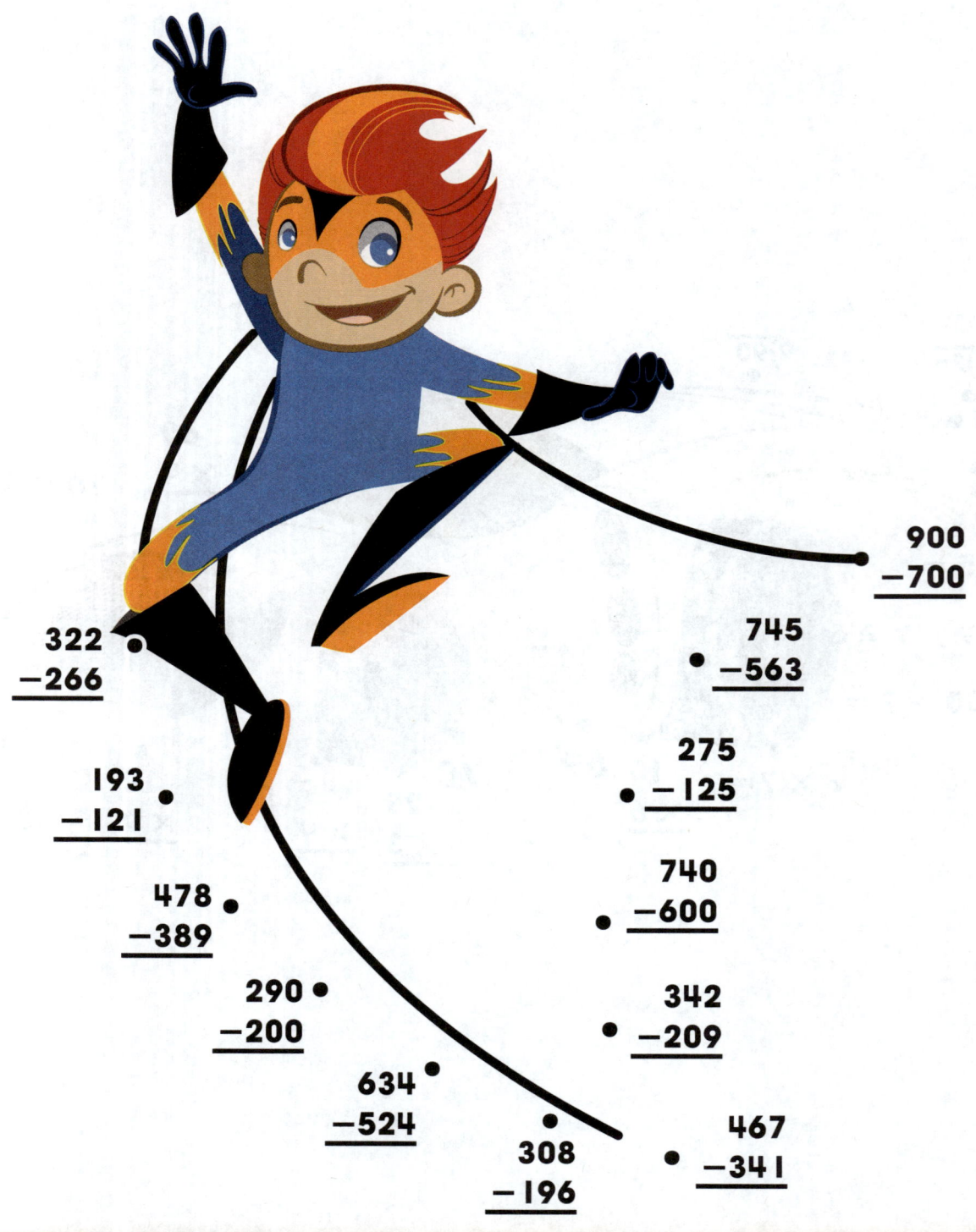

```
 900
-700
```

```
 322
-266
```

```
 745
-563
```

```
 275
-125
```

```
 193
-121
```

```
 478
-389
```

```
 740
-600
```

```
 290
-200
```

```
 342
-209
```

```
 634
-524
```

```
 308
-196
```

```
 467
-341
```

252   **SUPER SKILL POWERS • GRADE 3**

BONUS ACTIVITY

Finish the picture.

BONUS ACTIVITY

Finish the picture.

NAME _____

BONUS ACTIVITY

Finish the picture.

NAME _____

BONUS ACTIVITY

Finish the picture.

JOIN THE SUPERHERO TEAM!
DECORATE YOUR HERO WITH THE STICKERS YOU EARN!